D0560098

A Time to Conceal

A Time to Reveal

MOSAICA PRESS

ENLIGHTENING THOUGHTS ABOUT
PURIM AND CHANUKAH WITH HUMOR

RABBI YEHOSHUA KURLAND

Mosaica Press, Inc.

Designed and typeset by Brocha Mirel Strizower

ISBN-10: 1-946351-05-9
ISBN-13: 978-1-946351-05-0

Published and distributed by:
Mosaica Press, Inc.
www.mosaicapress.com
info@mosaicapress.com

Author can be reached at yhsk218@gmail.com.

THIS BOOK IS DEDICATED TO THE LOVING MEMORY OF OUR DEAR COUSIN AND EVERYONE'S BEST FRIEND

Mrs. Susan Sokol, a"h

זיסל עטיל בת יהושע שכנא ז״ל

She illuminated our lives and the lives of the multitudes of people who were *zocheh* to know her. With great humility before Hashem she touched their hearts with her warmth and penetrated their souls with her grace and nobility. Her approach was simple. She genuinely loved people and saw in them the image of Hashem. With *hachnasas orchim* that knew no bounds and *chesed* that was unending, she imitated her Creator who is "*mechayeh es kulam*" and infused life into others. She had a smile and good word for everyone and sagacious advice and counsel that provided astute guidance to all of her constituency. Her home in Chicago was the address for all who needed nourishment of the body and nurturing of the soul. Together with the unswerving dedication of, *yibadeil l'chaim tovim v'aruchim*, her legendary husband, Dr. Binyomin Sokol, both *kiruv rechokim* and *kiruv kerovim* permeated the aroma-filled atmosphere of their humble abode at 6634 N. Mozart. In truth, the famous composer didn't come close to producing the beautiful symphony that was the life and the legacy of this special person. The purity and holiness of her *eidele neshamah* was well concealed behind a mirage of the mundane and the routine, but there was nothing ordinary about this magnificent *eishes chayil* who was both aristocratic and regal. She truly followed in the footsteps of her saintly grandmother, Bubby Rissel Zelman, *z"l*, the matriarch of the Wolper, Schayer, Glenner, and Zelman families, an unusual *tzadekes* whose *deveikus* in Hashem was extraordinary. Like her Bubby, her love for Hashem and His Torah was exceptional, as she was always eager to hear a good *vort* or to open her *Tehillim*. Her greatest *nachas* was to see her children and grandchildren blossom into *b'nei* and *b'nos Torah* and, *baruch Hashem*, her dreams have seen fruition in families who are *bli ayin hara l'sheim u'l'tiferes b'Yisroel*.

Mrs. Sokol was a prime example of greatness and humility combined into one. She so naturally concealed that greatness with immense *tzenius*, but to those who knew her it was clearly revealed and admired, for her special *neshamah* shone through and through. She is sorely missed, for a person of this caliber can never be replaced.

It is therefore a privilege and honor to dedicate this volume, entitled *A Time to Conceal, A Time to Reveal* — which promotes the recognition of Hashem's ongoing *nisim* and *nifla'os* at all times, in all situations, both apparent and veiled — to one who personified that acknowledgment in every fiber of her being.

ת.נ.צ.ב.ה.

Letters of approbation for author's previous book, *A Time to Dance*

בס"ד

שמואל קמנצקי
Rabbi S. Kamenetsky

2018 Upland Way
Philadelphia, Pa 19131

Home: 215-473-2798
Study: 215-473-1212

כ"ז ניסן, תשע"ו

למע"כ מרביץ תורה יותר ממ' שנה בישיבת שאר ישוב ומקרב לבבות רחוקים וקרובים לאביהם שבשמים, ידידי הרב יהושע העשיל שמחה קורלאנד שליט"א, בן ידידי היקר הרב יעקב קורלאנד זצ"ל,

הגיעני החוברות בעניני שלום בית מספרו עת לרקוד שנכתב כל פרק ופרק בהקדמת מילתא דבדיחותא בתורת פתח לפתוח לבם של הקוראים על ידי פתיחת לבם מחמת השמחה להמוסר והעצות כדי שיבנו בית המיוסד על השלוה והשלום. וידוע לדאבונינו בזמנינו במיוחד כמה נחוץ הוא החזקת השלום בין איש לאשתו למענם ולמען משפחתם ואיך שמתוך השלום שורה השכינה בביתם.

ולכן באתי בברכה למע"כ הנ"ל שיצליח להשפיע על הרבים ויזכה לזכות את הרבים בספרים אחרים וימשיך לראות פירי פירות מכל עמלו בעזרת ה'.

המברכו בכל מילי דמיטב.

שמואל קמנצקי

בס"ד

מכתב ברכה

RABBI NAFTALI JAEGER
ROSH HAYESHIVA

יום ב' לס' ראה אנכי נותן לפניכם היום ברכה..." כ"ה אייר תשע"ג לפ"ק

בפרשת מתן תורה כתיב: כה תאמר לבית יעקב ותגיד לבני ישראל" ובגמ' (שבת פז.) כה תאמר. בלשון הזה כסדר הזה: לבית יעקב. אלו הנשים תאמר להן בלשון רכה: ותגיד לבני ישראל עונשין ודקדוקין פרש לזכרים דברים הקשין כגידין: ובגמ' (שבת פז.) רבי אומר בתחלה פירש עונשה דכתיב "ויגד משה" דברים שמושכין דעתו של אדם [illegible] ולבסוף פירש מתן שכרה דכתיב "ויגד משה" דברים שמושכין לבו של אדם כאגדה איכא דאמרי בתחלה פירש מתן שכרה דכתיב "ויגד משה" דברים שמגידין דעתו של אדם ולבסוף פירש עונשה דכתיב "ויגד משה" דברים שקשין לאדם כגידין. זה הוי דרכי ומנהגי אומני צריך לדעת איך ללמד ולמשוך ולהשפיע כל אחד לפי תכונתו [illegible] ובגמ' דומה (שבת ל:) כי הא דרבה. מקמי דפתח להו לרבנן אמר מילתא דבדיחותא ובדחי רבנן [illegible] בשמחה דשמעתא

[illegible] ידידי הנכבד הרה"ג רבי יהושע נ"י יאיר ויזרח בן [illegible] הבא"ג [illegible] מבחירי תלמידי הגאון האמיתי הגר"י [illegible] רודרמן [illegible] [illegible] ארבעים שנה [illegible] ונותן לו [illegible] [illegible] לחם ושמלה [illegible] [illegible] כסדרן לתלמידים [illegible] הרי הוא נותן [illegible] ויראת שמים [illegible] [illegible] [illegible] [illegible] להכניס את התורה [illegible] רבי שלמה פרייפלד זצללה"ה [illegible] [illegible] הכבוד [illegible] [illegible] לבו של אדם ומשיבין דעתו [illegible] לכל נפש והם דברים המושכין [illegible] [illegible] כל כוונתו הוא לשם שמים [illegible] [illegible] [illegible] [illegible] [illegible] בכל דרכיו [illegible]

הכותב מוקיר [illegible] התורה [illegible]

[illegible]

נפתלי הלוי יעגר

SH'OR YOSHUV

ONE CEDARLAWN AVENUE • LAWRENCE, NY 11559 • (516) 239-9002 • FAX (516) 239-9003

RABBI JOSEPH ROTTENBERG
3301 B TANEY ROAD
BALTIMORE MD 21215
410 578-8245

הרב יוסף נחמן ראטענבערג
ראש ישיבת חפץ חיים
באלטימאר

[illegible]

יוסף נחמן ראטענבערג

בס״ד

ZEEV HATORAH

Your Yeshiva in Jerusalem

Rav Shmuel Brazil, *Rosh HaYeshiva*

ח׳ ניסן תשע״ג

לכבוד ידידי היקר עד מאד משפיע ומרביץ תורה לרבים מוה״ר ר׳ יהושע נ״י

You have always been an inspirer of all ages, both men and women alike, facilitating their *Aliyah* in Torah and *Yiddishkeit* by using your געבענטש *chochmas haTorah*, warmth, and wit and sense of humor. Over the years working together as Rabbeim in Yeshivas Shor Yoshuv, I have constantly witnessed how your unique, engaging style and incredible demonstrative love for *Yidden*, nourished them to grow and to actualize their potential in becoming true *B'nei Torah* and *Ehrliche Baalei Batim* who are seriously *kovaiyah eetim* for *limud haTorah*. Hashem has given you a remarkable talent that during the same *Derasha*, you have literally caused your audience to shed tears through a heart rendering and riveting story or passionate point, soon to be followed by tears that flow from an uncontrollable laughter, having been embraced by your poignant humor together with your flawless delivery.

For making people happy and lifting up their spirits alone, one receives unfathomable *s'char* in Olam Habbah. We were both *zocheh* to hear our great Rebbe, Reb Shlomo *zt"l* relate on numerous occasions the Gemarah in *Taanis* that extols the virtues of the "two clowns," dubbing them "בני עלמא דאתי" However, when the humor is immediately followed by a message and a *Mussar*, then the reward is twofold. It is through the medium of Simcha that even the most stubborn heart can be pried open and is transformed into a receptacle to receive the *Mussar*, consequently inspiring the listener to committing in making a meaningful change in his life.

The Gemarah says that there are two ways to acquire an object: through lifting and through pulling (הגבהה and משיכה). Lifting is the superior method of acquisition. The *Middah* of *simchah* has the ability to lift off of one's heart all the heaviness, pressures, and disappointments that incessantly obstruct the entry of thoughts that motivate a spiritual awakening. However, once that burden is relieved, and one's Lev is accessible, penetrable, and open to listen, the Yid can acquire a *Yeshuah* by following a path toward self-improvement.

It is brought down that the author of a *sefer* should hint his name in its title. Rav Yehoshua (Heshel) Simcha, you need not bother since the entire contents of your *sefer* from beginning to end totally embodies your name. It is my humble *brachah* to you that each inspiring message and theme should bring about personal spiritual *yeshuos* and change in the lives of the readers through the powerful medium of *simchah*.

בברכה שתצליח לעורר לבות בנ״י לאביהם שבשמים

בידידות רבה בלב ובנפש

שמואל ברזיל

בס"ד

YESHIVA SHALOM RAV

P.O.Box 320, Sefat, Israel   Telefax: 9724-692-3643

shrshlom@netvision.net.il

www.shalomrav.org

Rabbi Rafael Weingot, Dean

כ"ד אייר תשע"ג

לכבוד ידידי היקר באדם, מוה"ר ר' יהושע, שליט"א.

בהקדמת אחי הקצות, מוהר"ר יהודי' הכהן זלה"ח לספר משובב נתיבות, מנמק טעמו שעמל ויגע להוציא ספרי אחיו הגדול לדפוס וז"ל: "וגם ידעתי את נפשו וגודל תשוקתו להפיץ חוצה מעייני חכמתו. כי כן דרך כל משכיל יתאוה להודיע לזולתו מכל מה שישיג וישכיל מעוצם בינתו. והרב מוהר"י מוסקאטו ז"ל כתב שאם הי' אפשר לאדם עלותו השמימה לראות בצבאות מעלה סדרם וישרם לא הי' מתענג בהשגתו עד שובו הנה לספר לחבריו את המראה הגדול ההוא ולהם יתן אומר המבשר צבא רב הגופים היקרים ההם עם פלאי פלאות נעשו במלאכתם הכי נכבדת."

אפשר להמליץ דבריו על מוה"ר ר' יהושע שליט"א שמתוך שהוא מבורך במאה כישרונות דהיינו בין בלימוד ובין בחינוך; בין בשירה וזמרה ובין בשפה ברורה ונעימה עם הבריות; בין ברות המוסר וחסידות ובין בבדיחות חריפות המשמחות לב אנשים; הרי הוא כנהר המלא על גדותיו שמוכרח לשפוך מי רויה על כל סביבותיו. מטבע הטוב להיטיב ומטבע לב מלא תורה חכמה ומוסר לשאוף להעניק לאחרים מאוצרו.

יעזרהו ה' להפיץ רעיונותיו חוצה ויהנו קטן וגדול מדברי תורתו המשמחות לב.

Rabbi Yehoshua Kurland has touched upon a key to awaken the Jewish soul-humor. Certainly he has learned this from our illustrious Rebbe, Rabbi Shlomo Freifeld, Zatzal, who was a master of delivering mussar through humor. To what he has learned he has added his own unique blend of humor and seriousness, good cheer and selfless dedication which are his trademark.

His ability to constantly give of himself to the Yeshiva and his talmidim is truly remarkable and a genetic trait of his illustrious family.

May ה' give him כח to find expression and fulfillment for the rare and subtle strivings of his sensitive נשמה.

ידידך,

רפאל וינגוט

Contents

Acknowledgments

WITH great thanks to Hashem, I humbly present this volume, *A Time to Conceal, A Time to Reveal*, essays on Purim and Chanukah, to the reading public. *Hakaras ha-tov* is unending, and with that in mind I thank the *Ribono Shel Olam* not only for allowing me the privilege to publish this book but for the seven that have preceded it during the course of the past seven years. Again, as in the past, I have begun each essay with a humorous story in the spirit of the classic *milsa d'bedichusa*, amusing matter, which hopefully will help open up the heart of the reader to the lesson at hand.

I would be remiss in writing a book about Purim and Chanukah to not make mention of the ongoing *nisim v'niflaos* that we are all *zocheh* to on a constant basis. On a personal level, there are not enough pages to accommodate the appreciation that my wife and my family feel for Hashem's great kindness. From the miraculous to the mundane, from the unnatural to the expected, it is all miraculous, and we endeavor to express our recognition of Hashem's eternal benevolence. May this volume inspire others to properly value the great miracle of life both *b'derech ha-teva* and *shelo b'derech ha-teva* and thank our Creator accordingly. Undoubtedly, the *nisim* of *ba-yamim ha-hem*, in those days continue to grace our existence *ba-zman ha-zeh*, in our day and age, for which we are infinitely grateful.

I will spare you the details of all of my acknowledgments, but suffice it to say I am grateful to my parents and in-laws, *zt"l*, my *rabbeim* and colleagues, my family and friends, my *talmidim* and *talmidos*, past and present, for their great contribution to my life in so many ways. To my children, there aren't words to properly express my love and admiration for every one of you, *bli ayin hara*. And, *acharon acharon chaviv*, to my wife, Leah, *shetichyeh*; I thank the *Ribono Shel Olam* for the great *zechus* to have merited such an *eishes chayil*. You have taught me so much. May we be *zocheh* to continue to stretch ourselves together *lema'an Hashem v'Toraso* in good health *ad bi'as goel tzedek*.

To my dear friends Seth and Zahavah Farbman: You have been more than friends. You have been available at all times, accessible and ready to be of assistance, anticipating our every need. I was embarrassed to even ask for your help to sponsor yet another Yehoshua Kurland book project, as I imagined you thinking: "Why does this Kurland guy have such a *yetzer hara* to write books?" Yet before I could get the words out of my mouth, you were there, affirmative and assenting, with great encouragement and excitement. Seth, you said, "Of course! It's a given!" I greatly appreciate your willingness to be a primary part of this endeavor, but I want you to know that I don't assume it as a "given," and I am filled with thanks and admiration. May your lives be filled with all of the blessings of Hashem and may you derive great *Torahdike nachas* from all of your wonderful children and future generations, *b'ezras Hashem*.

Much thanks and appreciation to my dear friends Jeff and Sharona Weinberg, Carmi and Katie Gruenbaum, and Yaakov and Michal Avigdor who have always given me much *chizuk* in this and in past endeavors. Your frienship is very meaningful to me and I feel privileged to enjoy such a relationship. May Hashem shower your lives with many *simchas* and continued *nachas* from all of your children.

A special thanks goes to a silent partner in this project. Refusing to allow me to reveal your identity and insisting that your major contribution remain anonymous, I nonetheless would be terribly negligent to not express my appreciation. You are an unusual person with great accomplishments. Hashem has blessed you with a multiplicity of talents and an uncanny ability to lead and to inspire with tremendous charm and charisma. May you be *zocheh* to continued *hatzlachah* and remarkable *simchas* and may your most generous effort to help promote this volume bring great *siyata d'shmaya* to see all of your hopes and dreams come to fruition!

To Rabbi Yaacov Haber, the publisher of Mosaica Press; to Rabbi Doron Kornbluth, the editor; to Mrs. Sherie Gross, managing editor; and to Mrs. Rayzel Broyde, art director; and to all of those engaged in the cooperative effort essential to the publication of a manuscript, your talent is exceptional and your *middos* impeccable. Thank you for all that you have done. May you be *zocheh* to continue your holy work of *harbatzas haTorah* through the medium of the printed word in good health for many years to come!

Purim and Chanukah are very much about the revelation of light and the unveiling of concealment. It is a time of masquerades and menorahs, reversal and enlightenment, *kabbalas haTorah* and a life-saving recovery of a threat of *shechichas haTorah* through the advent of *pilpulah shel Torah*, specifically the *Torah Sheba'al Peh*. Perhaps, most importantly, it is a time of a renewed *deveikus* in Hashem, inspired by an unequivocal recognition of Hashem's ever-presence and unremitting glory. It is a time when it is understood that there might seem to be a time when there is concealment and a time when there is revelation, but in truth they are one and the same, for there isn't a moment that transpires that isn't by virtue of the will of our Creator, and for this we are eternally grateful.

אין אנחנו מספיקים להודות לך ה' אלקינו ואלקי אבותינו
ולברך את שמך על אחת מאלף אלפי אלפים ורבי רבבות
פעמים הטובות שעשית עם אבותינו ועמנו.

Yehoshua Heshel Simcha Kurland
14 Marchesvan, 5777
Far Rockaway, NY

INTRODUCTION

THE Torah ordained that we celebrate the *Shalosh Regalim*, the three festivals of Pesach, Shavuos, and Succos. Purim and Chanukah share the distinction as the two Yamim Tovim that were established by the *rabbanan*. The miraculous intervention of the *yad Hashem* in both eras is the foundation of our celebration of these two holidays. *Megillas Taanis* records these days of Purim and Chanukah amongst a list of many days that share the distinction as days when miracles occurred. On these thirty-six occasions, two basic rules were to be observed: to not fast and (on some of them) to not deliver eulogies as well. When the Temple was destroyed, all of the days listed in *Megillas Taanis* were nullified except for these two. Only Purim and Chanukah remain from that list to be celebrated as days of joy and festivity, praise of Hashem, and thanksgiving. In a sense these two beloved events are infused with enough Divine illumination to supply sufficient light to allow us to traverse the difficult and dark path of the *galus* and cross the bridge to the days of the ultimate *geulah*.

Clearly, a common thread in both of these occasions is the celebration of Hashem's miracles. At times the *yad Hashem* is concealed and other times revealed, but at all times the extraordinary and miraculous is operating. Hashem is "*mechadeish b'tuvo b'chol yom tamid ma'aseh bereishis* — in His goodness He renews the creation every day."[1] Could there be a greater *nes* than the *hischadshus ha-olam*? We are told that we must praise Hashem for every breath. Because of the similarity between the

1 *Birchos Kriyas Shema.*

word *neshamah*, soul, and *neshimah*, breath, the *pasuk*, "*Kol haneshamah tehalel Kah* — All of the soul shall praise Hashem,"[2] is expounded to teach that one should praise Hashem *al kol neshimah u'neshimah* — for each and every breath. Is not man's ability to breathe anything less than miraculous? From the time that we awake in the morning until we retire for the evening — and while we sleep as well — we are a living miracle, constantly nurtured by the spectacular and phenomenal intervention of the Master of all miracles, Hashem. Were it not for the veneer of *teva*, nature, we would be exposed to the full glory of Hashem without any *tzimtzum*, contraction, and our freedom of choice would be obviated by the obvious presence of the Shechinah. Disguised or not, in truth Hashem's presence is all-encompassing. He is the *Mekomo Shel Olam*. He is everywhere at all times! Our task is to reveal the concealment and uncover His glory and celebrate *teva* and the miraculous as one colossal display of Hashem's omnipotence and ever-presence.

There are times when Hashem's *hanhagah*, conduct, is one of *hester*, disguise. It is often a response to our recalcitrance in our service of Him. When we conduct our lives *b'keri* — i.e., everything being coincidental, Hashem responds in the realm of *middah k'neged middah*, measure for measure, and appears *bachamas keri*, giving the impression that He has abandoned us. Our haphazard attitude is met with what appears to be a casual and inconsistent relationship, devoid of Hashem's uninterrupted *hashgachah*. Our failure to be *megaleh kavod Shamayim*, to reveal the glory of Hashem, could illicit a reaction of a facade of distance and detachment. One could feel lost, abandoned, and forsaken. Where is one to turn?

One response is to turn into one's very self and draw strength that one never knew he had. The instruction to Avraham Avinu to uproot himself from his father's land, "*Lech lecha* — Go for your good," was not only the first of the ten tests, but was the *modus operandi* for how to deal with such challenges. *Lech lecha*, go into yourself and uncover an untapped inner strength that will expand your ability to deal with the

2 *Tehillim* 150:6.

situation at hand. That is to say: reveal that which is concealed within, i.e., the *kochos hanefesh* that transcend all limitations and catapult a person to new horizons. This formula is a *yerushah*, an inheritance from our father Avraham, and has withstood the trials and tribulations of generations.

But there is another way. The more we whack away the weeds of interference, the spiritual plaque of a tunnel vision that refuses to recognize Hashem's ever-present *hashgachah*, the more Hashem will respond in kind and make His presence known. When we will trace everything that exists to the one source, i.e., Hashem; when we will abandon our notion of any haphazardness and focus on the truth of the unending, nonstop, interminable, and everlasting *hashgachah* of Hashem, then the miraculous will unveil itself and the hidden will become celebrated for the G-dliness that was always there.

On both Purim and Chanukah we were threatened by an enemy that struck at our core values. Whether it was the arrogance of an Amaleki who championed the world view of *mikreh* and was in defiance of a people whose laws were different, or the brazenness of the Yevanim who dared to suggest there could be a replacement for Torah, our eyes were darkened and our spirituality assaulted. But the courageous Mordechai and Esther, and the bold and gallant Chashmona'im, withstood the test, reached for their inner strengths, and tuned in to the oneness of Hashem and to the oneness of His Torah. Our relationship with Hashem is never haphazard and our Torah is never replaceable. And sure enough the *yeshuah* came, the miraculous surfaced, and the enemy was defeated. The concealed was revealed for what it always was and always is, and the *teva* was removed before our very eyes. The light of Torah shone brilliantly in the menorah, and to the Jews of Shushan there was *orah*, *simchah*, *sason*, and *yekar* — *ken tihyeh lanu*, so shall it continue for all generations until the time when we will finish the unfinished symphony with a jubilant song at the *chanukas ha-mizbeiach b'binyan Beis HaMikdash u'b'vias ha-Mashiach, bimheirah b'yamenu, Amen*!

Part I: Purim

A Time to Conceal

CHAPTER 1

LOOK BEFORE YOU LEAP

HASHEM IS NEVER MISSING.
HE IS ALWAYS LEADING THE WAY.

There was a famous doctor, an old man, and a boy scout on an airplane that was experiencing engine failure. Unfortunately, there were only two parachutes. The quick-thinking but somewhat arrogant doctor stated: "I am the smartest man here and most essential to the world," so he quickly grabbed one of the two and promptly jumped out!

The old man turned to the boy scout and said, "My time has been good and the end is near. You have a long life ahead of you, so go on, kid."

The boy scout replied, "No, that's okay; there is a parachute for each of us. The smartest man in the world was in such a hurry that he just jumped out with my knapsack."

THERE was a time when man could see from one end of the world to the other — from the earth to the heavens. Since the famous sin of Adam HaRishon, man's vision has dramatically diminished.

Nonetheless, at times, through advances in one's *avodas Hashem*, he is capable of piercing the veil that hides the true glory of Hashem. With clarity, we can visualize worlds that are light years beyond this one. These lucid moments do not come often but they do come. At those times, even the most stalwart and stubborn person can see through the façade that reveals Hashem's ubiquitous omnipresence.

The truly wise man understands that, indeed, he understands very little, and he takes a good hard look at the world before him and beyond him before he takes that leap of faith that could prove frivolous and futile. The *chacham's* eyes are *b'rosho*, on top of his head, not only perceiving the repercussions of his actions, but also peering into the abstract to remove the barriers and reveal the truth about the ever-presence of Hashem.

Megillas Esther is the classic representation of this exposure of Hashem's presence from what appeared to be the epitome of hiddenness. The very expression "*megillas Esther*" makes this abundantly clear: *megillah* is an expression of *gilui*, revelation, and *Esther* is an expression of *hester*, hiddenness, so the phrase becomes "the revelation from the hiddenness." The many layers of plaque of aberration are hacked away (*megillah* is also an expression of *magal*, a sickle) as the story unfolds, and Hashem's master plan of salvation evolves. Ultimately, it becomes unequivocally clear that Hashem's name — which does not appear throughout the *Megillah* — is in fact well represented by virtue of the bountiful times it mentions the word *melech*, which serves as an allusion to Him.

More importantly, the *Megillah* represents the revelation of G-d's glory as our eyes are opened to the reality that indeed His glory fills the entire world — and the entire storyline from beginning to end.

This revelation was so dramatic that it impacted the hearts of the Jews with an overwhelming love for Hashem and His Torah, inspiring a reacceptance of the Torah with a passion that surpassed their enthusiasm at Har Sinai. No longer was there a disclaimer that "You forced us to acquiesce by lifting the mountain over our heads and threatening our lives with 'either you accept the Torah or *sham tehei kevuraschem* — there you will be buried.'" The "excuse" was *batul*, null and void. The unequivocal awareness that Hashem is never missing and is leading the way even in what appears to be the darkest of times left an indelible impression upon Klal Yisrael, then and forever.

Were we to see the true glory of Hashem at all times, we would lose our *bechirah*, our freedom of choice; we would lose the greatest gift ever given to mankind — the privilege of choosing spirituality and the merit that evolves from overcoming obstacles and emerging victorious. This "forces" the *Ribono Shel Olam* to disguise Himself and at times feign that He "goes into hiding." It is our task in life to uncover the glory of Hashem from its invisibility and to restore it to its crown of majesty.

When we do that, it will be Purim every day!

CHAPTER 2

NON-BELIEVERS FINISH LAST

EMUNAH IN HASHEM SHAPES MIRACLES.

A young female teacher with obvious liberal tendencies explains to her class of small children that she is an atheist. She asks her class if they are atheists too. Not really knowing what atheism is, but wanting to be like their teacher, their hands explode into the air like fleshy fireworks.

There is, however, one exception. A girl named Sarah does not go along with the crowd. The teacher asks her why she has decided to be different.

"Because," she protests. "I'm not an atheist."

The teacher then asks, "What are you?"

"I'm a Jew," she exclaims.

The teacher is a little perturbed now, her face slightly red. She asks Sarah why she is a Jew.

"Well, I was brought up knowing and loving Judaism. My mom is a Jew, and my dad is a Jew, so I am a Jew."

The teacher is now angry. "That's no reason to embrace

Judaism," she says loudly. "What if your mom was a moron and your dad was a moron. What would you be then?"

She paused, and smiled. "Then," says Sarah, "I'd be an atheist."

BELIEF in Hashem is obviously imperative to all that we hold sacred. The Gemara at the end of *Makkos* states that already in the days of the prophet Chabakuk, the 613 mitzvos (each of which has its own premise and emphasis) were "reduced" to just one *yesod*, foundation. That principle is: "*Tzaddik b'emunaso yichyeh* — The righteous live through their faith (in G-d)."[3] For that generation, and most certainly for ours today, the basis of our observance depends on our *emunah*. This does not exempt us from the performance of all 613 mitzvos, and we remain absolutely obligated in spite of our inability to recognize each mitzvah's precise *yesod*. The point of the Gemara is that *emunah* is to be the focus of our mitzvah performance. Indeed, every mitzvah is interlinked with the 612 others,[4] but the *yesod* of *emunah* remains as the ever-present notion in our lives of observance.

Peculiarly, the expression used to describe that Mordechai raised Esther is not the typical *higdil*, he raised. Instead, the *Megillah* tells of Mordechai's nurturing of Esther as the guardian of his orphaned relative (according to some opinions, as her husband as well) with an expression that implies *emunah*: "*Vayehi* ***omen*** *es Hadassah hi Esther bas dodo asher ein lah av v'em* — And he raised Hadassah; she was Esther his cousin who had no parents."[5]

The pious Esther, the heroine of the Purim story who dared go to the king uninvited to plead for the salvation of her people, was a product of the *emunah* in HaKadosh Baruch Hu that was instilled in her from an early age by Mordechai. We see that *emunah*, an expression of training for a craft, doesn't simply "happen." It is a result of

---

3 *Makkos* 24a.

4 As we say in the *l'shem yichud* that many recite before performing a mitzvah: *v'es taryag mitzvos hateluyos bah*.

5 *Esther* 2:7.

years of schooling — a consequence of solid *chinuch*. It is something ingrained from one's youth and reinforced by overcoming challenges that threaten its viability. A child whose parents immediately proclaim *Baruch Hashem yom yom* — Hashem is to be blessed every day — to all situations that life offers absorbs this faith, one that in the case of Esther served her well and gave her the impetus and the fortitude to valiantly save Klal Yisrael. There is no doubt that these *tzaddikim* lived with an *emunah* for which we are the grateful beneficiaries.

Chapter 3

Turnabout

Salvation Sewn in Obliteration

One day, a boy saw a farmer selling a donkey for a hundred dollars. The boy told the farmer he would pay the money up front if the farmer could deliver it to his house. The farmer agreed to deliver the donkey the next day, but when he arrived at the boy's house, he was empty-handed. There was no donkey. He told the boy that the donkey died during the night. Saddened, the boy asked for his money back.

"I'm afraid I have already spent the money." the farmer said.

"Well, then just give me the donkey," said the boy.

"What are you going to do with a dead donkey?" asked the farmer. The boy told the farmer he would think of something, so the farmer delivered the donkey the next day.

The next month the farmer saw the boy and asked him what he ever did with the donkey.

"I made $895 off that thing," the boy said.

"How could you make that much money off of a dead donkey?" the farmer wanted to know.

The boy said, "I didn't tell anyone he was dead at first. I just put up signs around town that said I was going to raffle off a beautiful donkey for raffle tickets that cost five dollars and I sold 200 tickets."

"Wait a minute," said the farmer, "you said you made $895. But if you sold 200 tickets at five dollars each, that's $1,000. After you subtract the $100 you paid me, you should have made $900."

"You're right," said the boy. "But when the winner found out the donkey was dead, he was so upset I gave him his five dollars back."

IT is quite impressive when an astute businessman can turn a profit. It takes quite a sharp and shrewd entrepreneur to somehow utilize the very vehicle for the fiscal disaster of others as the precise medium for his success. I am reminded of a dear friend's father who singlehandedly turned the 1929 stock market crash (which was the financial ruin of millions of people) into an opportunity to make millions of dollars. This man lived to the ripe age of 104, building his financial empire until his end.

The Gemara in *Makkos* uses the expression "*vehi hanosenes*" to convey the idea that the very reason you thought was the underlying foundation of your logic is actually the precise reason for your error.[6] Let's explore this crucial idea.

The Gemara says: One might naturally think that the requirement of exile to the cities of refuge for one who kills unwittingly is to be understood as a punishment. Therefore, it follows that if the *meizid* (one who kills deliberately but was not warned) who actually **performed an act** of murder (a *ma'aseh*) doesn't need to uproot himself and run there, then certainly the plotting witnesses (*eidim zomemim*) who merely **attempted** to have someone killed but were apprehended beforehand (and never did an actual deed) shouldn't be subject to exile. In other words, they did less than the *meizid* did and therefore should be punished less.

To this argument, the Gemara counters with *vehi hanosenes* — quite to the contrary! *Galus*, exile, is not a punishment as much as it is a *kaparah*,

6 *Makkos* 2b.

an atonement! Therefore, the very fact of not having done an actual deed is the precise reason people are eligible for that *kaparah*. In contrast, the one who killed deliberately without warning is undeserving of this atonement. Thus, the very factor cited as a reason to consider false witnesses less fit for the penalty of *galus* (i.e., their inactivity) is the very reason to consider *galus* a more plausible consequence for their crime.

We are often fooled to believe we understand the events of our lives. The many *vehi hanosenes* moments begin to accrue as we mature in our understanding of the greatness of the Master Planner, the *Ribono Shel Olam*, and the unfathomable symphony of His creation. What we thought was bad is all good, and what we thought was a hopeless situation is the very cause of our salvation. As mere *basar v'dam*, flesh and blood, we are small-minded and limited in our vision.

Purim is called so *al shem hapur* — because of the lots that were drawn to determine the day of doom for Klal Yisrael. To think that the great revelation that took place on Purim has any connection whatsoever to lotteries or pot luck is the greatest of parodies. Haman rejoiced as it fell out in Adar, the month of the demise of Moshe Rabbeinu. He failed to realize that it was also the month in which Moshe was born!

The irony of the entire Purim story is uncanny. The paradox of salvation sewn in obliteration and deliverance in destruction is a combination of many *vehi hanosenes* moments woven into an amazing miracle *al pi derech ha-teva*. This had a major impact on Klal Yisrael and inspired them to reaccept the Torah with an unadulterated *ahavah* and made its mark in history as the Yom Tov of all Yamim Tovim; as the Yom Tov that will be celebrated eternally; as the Yom Tov most associated with *acharis ha-yamim*, the end of time.

There is reason for that. The story of Purim serves as a prime example of a time characterized by an unequivocal recognition of the ever-presence of the *hashgachah* of Hashem in every aspect of our existence. Nothing is left to chance; nothing is haphazard. Even when things look bad, we must never forget that "*vehi hanosenes*" and we hopefully will merit to see all of the good in the Divine plan, as the *yeshuah*, a case in progress, will come imminently.

CHAPTER 4

FREE OF DEBT

THE DUAL DELIVERANCE OF PURIM IS CAUSE FOR MUCH CELEBRATION.

A young man was walking through a supermarket to pick up a few things when he noticed an old lady following him around. Thinking nothing of it, he ignored her and continued on. Finally, he went to the checkout line, but she pushed in front of him.

"Pardon me," she said, "I'm sorry if my staring at you has made you feel uncomfortable. It's just that you look just like my son, who died recently."

"I'm very sorry," replied the young man, "is there anything I can do for you?"

"Yes," she said, "As I'm leaving the store, can you say 'Good bye, Mother!'? It would make me feel so much better."

"Sure," answered the young man.

After the old woman checked out and was leaving the store, he called out, "Goodbye, Mother!"

His items were then scanned and he was told that his total was $127.50.

"How can it be so much?" he asked the clerk. "I only purchased a few things!"

The clerk responded, "Your mother said that you would pay for her too."

AS the bills pile up endlessly, we would all welcome some mysterious benefactor who would pick up the tab and clean the slate. It cannot be pleasant to be forced to declare bankruptcy. Yet, on the flip side, becoming free of debt is refreshing and rejuvenating. There is a joy in paying one's debts, as evidenced by the opinion in the Gemara in *Avodah Zarah* that a Jew may not accept the payment of a debt owed to him by an idol worshipper within three days of the idol worshipper's festival for fear that the elation he feels in becoming debt-free will inspire him to worship and thank his *avodah zarah*.[7]

One of the most euphoric moments one experiences during the course of the year is the exhilaration of Motzaei Yom Kippur. After forty days of *teshuvah*, *selichos*, and supplications; after more than twenty-four hours of fasting and holiness, the sea of white assembled in many a *kehillah*, clad in their *kittels* and *taleisim*, break into song and dance. Hunger and thirst subside as *neshamos* that have shed their liability, blessed with a clean slate, burst forth in ecstasy. In the Aish Kodesh Congregation in Woodmere, New York, where I am privileged to serve as the *baal tefillah*, the celebration can go on for close to half an hour!

The message is clear. There is no greater joy than the joy of *hataras hasefekos*, the unraveling of doubts.[8] We are once again sure and confident about our relationship with Hashem as He so graciously has accepted our *teshuvah*. We have a new lease on life. We are free to once again begin in our endeavor to serve Him as we should. We have humbly declared spiritual bankruptcy and are ready to rebuild.

Yom Kippur and Purim are linked together by Chazal. By translating the *kof* of *kippur* as a prefix meaning "like," the very name of the holiest day of the year, Yom Kippur[im], is understood as *Yom k'Purim*, a day

7 *Avodah Zarah* 2a.

8 *Metzudas David* to *Mishlei* 15:30.

like Purim. In fact, it is said in the name of the Vilna Gaon that they are really one Yom Tov divided into two:[9]

- Yom Kippur represents the *bechinah*, realm, of *chatzi laShem* — the part of a festival dedicated toward service of Hashem
- Purim is the realm of *chatzi lachem* — the part of a festival dedicated to one's physical self.

Added to the jubilance of the *nisim v'niflaos* that brought about our salvation and the revelation of the glory of Hashem unveiled from its mirage of hiddenness was the spiritual ecstasy of a nation whose *teshuvah* had been accepted and was enabled to begin again with a fresh start. It is no wonder that this day stands out as the epitome of all celebration, as it marks a dual deliverance of the physical and the spiritual.

Let us celebrate in body and soul as we anticipate a renewal in our dedication to our Father in Heaven, the *Melech Malchei HaMelachim, HaKadosh Baruch Hu*. Indeed, there is much reason for rejoicing.

---

9 *Likutei HaGr"a* (Warsaw), pg. 308.

CHAPTER 5

MAIN EVENT

WE DARE NOT CONFUSE THE MAIN COURSE WITH THE LURE OF THEIR WORLD.

The shopkeeper was dismayed when a brand new business much like his own opened up to his left and erected a huge sign that read BEST DEALS.

He was horrified when another competitor opened up on his right and announced its arrival with an even larger sign, reading LOWEST PRICES.

The shopkeeper was panicked until he got an idea. He put the biggest sign of all over his own shop. It read...MAIN ENTRANCE.

NOBODY likes a side show. Who wouldn't take seats behind home plate if he could get them? We are typically drawn to the main entrance, the glitter, and the lights. And so it was in Shushan. Achashverosh threw lavish parties. All were invited to partake; each person was personally catered to. His intent was to win over the masses — something like the many government handouts today. He knew that if he opened up the main entrance of his palace and all of its impressive ballrooms to the populace, they would be drawn near and this would guarantee him their allegiance. They fell for it — the Jews as well.

It wasn't the first time and it won't be the last. The temptation will always be there until we come to our senses and appreciate what we have and how everything else is miniscule in comparison. The true palace is the palace of the King of all kings. The greatest delicacy is Torah and mitzvos. The most dependable alliance is one that is built with Hashem. The ultimate event is *Olam Haba*, with this world merely acting as a corridor and gateway to enable entry into the main entrance at the gates of eternity.

It happened in Shushan, it happened in Germany, it's happening today in America, and depending on which direction you go in Yerushalayim Ir Hakodesh, you can see the same selling-out, the same misplaced priorities, the same mistaken notion that everything that they value, from lifestyle to liberalism, from hedonism to *hefkerus*, utter abandonment, is inviting and engaging. In contrast, the Jew of yesteryear longed for nothing but a *blatt Gemara*, a *perek Tehillim*, an opportunity to do *chesed*, a *deveikusdike niggun*, and a *shaychus* with the *Ribono Shel Olam*.

And even when we come to our senses and establish a hierarchy of priorities, we are not satisfied unless we can have it all. Torah is great, Shabbos is *geshmak*, mitzvos are worthwhile — but only when they come in a state-of-the-art package with all of the trimmings. It must be the perfect *shiur*, a brand-new *sefer*, the most expensive dinnerware and linens, ostentatious chandeliers and candelabras, and a *dirah* in Eretz Yisrael (providing, of course, that the new villa has a gorgeous view). I sense such flawed thinking among Jews who value Torah and who appreciate mitzvos but allow their prerequisite for a state-of-the-art package with all the trimmings to be equally as important. I'm sure that at times I am guilty of the same and get lost in this desire for "the best." It seems to be an unfortunate sign of the times.

However, this misses the point. It's easy to fall into the trap of the pursuit of *gashmius* "for the sake of *ruchnius*." It's so easy to profess altruism and nationalism when it is no more than a desire for acceptance into their world. Politicians in Israel are willing to release the worst murderers in order to gain favor and recognition in the eyes of the very people who are our avowed enemies. Such is the draw to enter their world. The examples get worse when we are drawn into their decadence and licentiousness. The celebration of Purim was one of Klal Yisrael coming to its senses and the unequivocal recognition of proper priorities.

The Sfas Emes said it perhaps best: The Gemara *darshens* the *pasuk* of "*LaYehudim haisah orah v'simchah v'sason v'yekar* — to the Jews there was light and happiness, joy and honor," in accordance with Klal Yisrael's renewed enchantment with Torah and mitzvos: *orah* is referring to Torah, *simchah* to Yom Tov, *sason* is *bris milah*, and *yekar* is *tefillin*.[10] The Sfas Emes asks the question we would all have loved to ask but wouldn't dare to: if that's what the *pasuk* meant, why didn't it write, "*LaYehudim haisah Torah, v'Yom Tov, umilah, utefillin*"?

He answers that it does, in fact, say just that! Klal Yisrael had such clarity as to their priorities that it was unequivocal that the only light was Torah, the only *simchah* was Yom Tov, the only *sason* was *bris milah*, and the only *yekar* was *tefillin* — the joy was synonymous with the mitzvah itself! Such was the clarity of a nation that went from utter despair to absolute faith and *deveikus*. They were *tofes es ha-ikar* and *meniach es ha-tafel* — they grabbed on to the primary and let go of the insignificant in the most magnificent way.

May we be *zocheh* to do the same so that we will, in turn, merit entering the main entrance of the eternal world with our priorities leading the way!

---

10 *Megillah* 16b.

CHAPTER 6

BELIEF IN THE UNBELIEVABLE

HE WHO TRUSTS IN HASHEM WILL BE SURROUNDED BY HIS KINDNESS.

Nine-year-old Joey was asked by his mother what he had learned in Sunday School. "Well, our teacher told us how G-d sent Moses behind enemy lines on a rescue mission to lead the Israelites out of Egypt. When he got to the Red Sea, he had his engineers build a pontoon bridge, and all the people walked across safely. He used his walkie-talkie to radio headquarters and call in an air strike. They sent in bombers to blow up the bridge and all the Israelites were saved."

"Now, Joey, is that REALLY what your teacher taught you?" his mother asked.

"Well no, Mom, but if I told it the way the teacher did, you'd never believe it."

TRUTH be told, if we needed everything to conform to human understanding and rationale, we would renounce half the stories in *Tanach*. Without strong *emunah* in Hashem and staunch *emunas chachamim*, our approach to much of our tradition would drown in a sea of skepticism. Unfortunately, many have indeed chosen that path of disbelief, demanding intellectual validation to all events or choosing to denounce such events as too abstract and intangible. What follows is often a total disregard for Torah and mitzvos and a desertion of religiosity. When left up to our own fallacious determination, the inclination to rationalize kicks in and the tendency for human error is blaring, although unnoticed by the protagonists of such a self-worship philosophy. In recent times, those who profess global warming to be the most important issue the world faces (in spite of the absence of absolute proof to their theory) have been exposed as manipulators of statistics and scientific facts. By making it their creed of life, they are blinded to their self-orientation in defiance of all integrity. In the process, their insistent attitude blocks any consideration to the limitations of man's understanding of such phenomena and curtails their connection to Hashem's eternal world of "*Ha'yipalei m'Hashem davar* — Is there anything that is beyond the ability of G-d"?

It's worse than that. The very power to bring about miracles lies in the degree of one's belief in the all-encompassing *yad Hashem*, hand of G-d. The *pasuk* promises: "*V'habote'ach b'Hashem chesed yesovevenhu* — And one who trusts in Hashem will be surrounded by His kindness."[11] This axiom is simply a measure-for-measure reward for our absolute faith in the truth of Hashem's goodness, His desire to bestow benefit upon us, and His absolute ability to do so. The more we believe it, the more we bring it to fruition. The skeptic eradicates his very own power to impact miraculous change. Were it not for the steadfast conviction of Mordechai that *tefillah* and repentance could alter the evil decree, we would have been doomed. Instead, he encouraged Esther to trust in Hashem and told her in no uncertain terms that if she refuses to go to Achashverosh, "*revach v'hatzalah ya'amod laYehudim m'makom acher* — the salvation will come from some other source other than you,"[12] but

11 *Tehillim* 32:12.

12 *Esther* 4:14.

it will come. Mordechai was *omed b'nisayon*; he withstood the test, took the bull by the horns, and did what he had to do to inspire miracles. It is no wonder that the Hebrew word for challenge, *nisayon*, finds its root in *nes*, miracle. Addressing *nisyonos* with absolute *bitachon* is the very formula that initiates a supernatural response from Heaven. The steadfast belief in the omnipotence of Hashem, in a sense, empowers Him in the spirit of *t'nu oz l'Elokim*, give strength to G-d, and enables Him to reveal His true colors to our great delight — and to the delight of all of mankind — perhaps with the exception of Haman and his cronies!

CHAPTER 7

BULL'S EYE

ONE SHOULD STRIVE FOR PERFECTION IN SPIRITUALITY, NOT IN EARTHLINESS.

Q: Why are there no Walmarts near the shooting range?
A: Because there are Targets everywhere.

WITH the emergence of the superstore, the store that has everything, one-stop shopping has become the way to go. From Walmart and Target to Home Depot and Loews, from clothing to toothpaste, from appliances to matches, it's all there under one roof. If it's bulk you want, Costco, BJs, and Sam's Club are there to serve you with commercial quantities at wholesale prices. Even the kosher consumer is treated to a variety of all-kosher supermarkets that cater to his or her every whim: meat, fish, baked goods, pizza, appetizers, and even sushi (!) — in addition to a plethora of groceries — all available for our convenience. Gone are the relationships with the grocer and the butcher, the fruit-and-vegetable man, and the fish monger. We don't even have to wait in line or deal with the checkout person; we can do self-checkout and be gone. Without having to say "please" or "thank you," we're on our merry way with everything we need in our basket.

Could anything be better?

There's a downside to such convenience. We become accustomed to living a life where everything is at our fingertips. It becomes an expectation. Years ago, they told the humorous story of the journalist who was interviewing people, asking them, "Excuse me, how do you feel about the meat shortage?" The Russian fellow said, "What is meat?" The American answered, "What is a shortage?" And the Israeli answered, "What is 'excuse me'?"

Thankfully, many of us have grown up never having to endure any shortages whatsoever. At the same time, we've been overly indulged, and even when not, we've been clothed and fed with abundance, and entertained with little lacking. In the process. we have become needy and dependent, and we have lost many of our coping skills, often making it difficult for us to adjust to the inevitable vicissitudes of the roller coaster of life. It incapacitates our need to fix things and realize that not everything is perfect. Worse than that, we put all of our efforts toward perfection in the wrong world — the world of *gashmius*.

One summer, we purchased gifts for our children in a store in the Geulah section of Yerushalayim. As the proprietor wrapped them, I noticed a piece of Scotch tape that had folded, detracting from the neatness of the package. Not wishing to bother him to re-wrap it, I simply asked him if I could have another piece of tape. He understood why I wanted it and in the nicest way proceeded to give me a whole schmooze on the topic of how everything in life is not perfect (only in Eretz Yisrael can you get a *mussar* schmooze in a gift shop!). Needless to say, he was on the mark, and it was I who was getting too wrapped up (excuse the pun) in the trappings.

I once presented one of my previously published books, *A Time to Laugh, A Time to Listen* to the Philadelphia Rosh Yeshiva, Harav Shmuel Kamenetsky, *shlit"a*. I wrote an inscription in the first volume and wrapped it in nice wrapping paper. Upon handing it to Rav Shmuel, who graciously accepted it, he neatly unwrapped it and handed the wrapping paper back to me, remarking: "It's a shame to waste the paper." If there is anyone who has his priorities clear, it is the Rosh Yeshiva!

What does all of this have to do with Purim? Everything! The participation of the *Yidden* in Achashverosh's "*fleish*-fest" was the straw that broke the camel's back. It was the catalyst for the terrible decree. Achashverosh's party was not simply lavish and over-the-top; it epitomized perfection. Everything had to be "just right." The detailed description of every nuance in the first chapter of *Megillas Esther* is not to encourage a career in party planning but rather to point out the temptation that proved to be Klal Yisrael's undoing. The feast of that *rasha* represents an attitude that prevails today. Unfortunately, it is not restricted to the non-Jewish world. It is one of extravagance to the point of the need for flawlessness. When a Jew is striving for *shleimus*, perfection, in materialism and not spirituality; when it must be the perfect wallpaper, the perfect kitchen cabinets, the perfect light fixture, the perfect jewelry, and the perfect linens and carpets, then we have grossly distorted our priorities and returned to the feast of Achashverosh. We need to get them straight. We need to be on target — not *in* Target! We need to have a paradigm shift and make a major reversal in our "perfection" focus. What better time for reversal than Purim? Let us take full advantage.

CHAPTER 8

SELF-WORSHIP

SELF-IDOLIZATION — THE GREATEST FORM OF AVODAH ZARAH

A man suffered a serious heart attack and had an open-heart bypass surgery. He awakened from the surgery to find himself in the care of nuns at a Catholic hospital.

As he was recovering, a nun asked him questions regarding how he was going to pay for his treatment. She asked if he had health insurance.

He replied in a raspy voice, "No health insurance."

The nun asked if he had money in the bank.

He replied "No money in the bank."

The nun asked, "Do you have a relative who could help you?"

He said, "I only have an old spinster sister who is a nun."

The nun became agitated and announced loudly, "Nuns are not spinsters! Nuns are married to G-d."

The patient replied, "Oh! Then send the bill to my brother-in-law."

WE are not foolish enough to believe the drivel of a Gentile world that maintains nonsensical assertions about G-d, such as being married to Him or "borne" of Him or of His flesh, *chalilah*. We dare not think of Him as an equal or anything of the like. And although the *pasuk* says "*Kedoshim tihyu*,"[13] and the Midrash comments: "*Yachol kamoni* — One might think that means just like Me (implying equality)," that is simply the *hava amina*, the preconceived notion. The Midrash ends with: "*Talmud lomar 'ki kadosh ani'* — The *pasuk* teaches otherwise, saying 'for I am holy.'"[14] Your holiness will never equal mine. Hashem is unfathomable and ubiquitous, omniscient and omnipresent.

Yet, our relationship to Hashem certainly should be one of great *deveikus* and attachment. We were created in His image and possess within us a *tzelem Elokim*, the very image of G-d that is a *chelek Elokah mi-ma'al*. Dovid HaMelech assured us: "*Hashem tzilcha al yad yeminecha* — Hashem is your shadow on your right side,"[15] a clear indication of the remarkable connection between a *Yid* and the *Ribono Shel Olam*. In a sense, the entire goal of the study of Torah and the performance of its mitzvos is precisely this *deveikus*. Torah and mitzvos are the glue that connects Klal Yisrael to their Creator. The holy words of the Zohar HaKadosh say it best: "*Yisrael v'Oraisah v'Kudshah Brich Hu, chad hu* — the Jewish people, and the Torah, and Hashem are one."[16]

The trials one faces to achieve this *deveikus* are many, especially in the climate of our world today. In contradistinction to years ago (when the inundation of the various *yetzer hara*s, although always present, was not as penetrating), today we face a barrage of *yetzer hara*s that are both all-pervading and seemingly inescapable. They do not merely present temptation, but make it very easy for one to become addicted hook, line, and sinker; before one knows it, he is *aduk v'davuk*, steadfastly attached. Any possible attachment to Hashem (*l'havdil elef havdalos*) is so easily replaced with a *deveikus* of promiscuity and licentiousness (*Hashem yerachem*).

This attachment to such debauchery is reminiscent of the *avodah zarah* of Baal Peor. In spite of the disgraceful method of its worship (which

13 *Vayikra* 19:2.

14 *Vayikra Rabbah* 24:9.

15 *Tehillim* 121:5.

16 *Zohar* 3:73/3.

included disrobing and defecating in front of the idol), it became popular even among Jews. Some of its most devoted worshippers were Jews. How such ignominy was a means of servitude to a supposed deity is mind-boggling! What could possibly draw a people of nobility to such disgrace?

In his inimitable style, Harav Chaim Shmuelevitz, *zt"l*, gets to the core of the matter: The worship of Baal Peor was not idol worship as much as it was self-worship. It was the worship of total abandonment; the worship of *hefkerus*. I can do anything I want, when I want, where I want, and before the entire world if I want. I can even do this despicable act in front of my deity for there is no "higher authority." It's all about me! We see echoes of this today, with Western culture less and less embarrassed by...anything at all.

It is no wonder that it was as attractive and alluring to have drawn the active participation of even *Yidden*, as it defied all authority and allowed the unbridling of all restraints. It was a declaration to the world that anything goes and we don't care. All we really care about is hedonism and self-gratification. In a sense, it was idol worship of the highest accord — the idolizing of oneself.

Haman Harasha and Hitler and others like them, *yemach shemam*, were guilty of such self-worship even if it wasn't of the Baal Peor variety. Haman didn't need the idol as an excuse for his self-worship. His delusions of grandeur, arrogance, and pure megalomania led him on his monstrous path without the *avodah zarah shebo*. He made himself into the *avodah zarah*. Indeed, his debasement and downfall began with a pail of waste products thrown upon him by his own daughter as he led Mordechai on the royal horse of the king. Perhaps this serves as a *remez*, a clue, to the Baal Peor idol he created out of his very being.

It serves as well as a warning to Klal Yisrael that it dare not declare its independence from the dictates of the Torah and pursue a life of *hefkerus*, for such self-worship could *chas v'shalom* be the catalyst to unleash upon them the likes of a Haman Harasha. Let us endeavor to remove ourselves from an attachment to a lifestyle that will inevitably lead to self-worship and instead humble ourselves before Hashem and cleave to Him with all of our soul.

Chapter 9

Anesthetized

Feeling the pain of others leads to salvation.

A New York couple was very frustrated that a severe toothache forced them to interrupt their upstate vacation soon after their arrival in order to return to the city to seek out a dentist.

Quite aggravated that their vacation had been disturbed, upon reaching the dentist, the woman blurted out: "I want this tooth pulled immediately, and I don't want any Novocaine because I'm in a big hurry. Just extract the tooth as quickly as possible and we'll be on our way," she demanded.

The dentist was quite impressed. "You're certainly a courageous woman," he said. "Which tooth is it?"

The woman turned to her husband and said, "Show him your tooth, dear."

ALL too often, we are fine with pain — as long as it isn't our own. When we are not the one suffering, our pain threshold is elevated and our endurance and tolerance levels are remarkably forbearing. I often wonder whether many doctors actually understand the degree of pain and discomfort patients experience through the procedure or treatment. Whereas *tzaddikim* of yesteryear would feel the pain of others, often breaking down in bitter tears, we have become hard-nosed and toughened. We are too easily apathetic and stoic in our response, at best offering a *kvetch* or a groan.

Chazal called the sensitivity that one should feel for his friend's plight *nosei b'ol chavero*, he helps to carry his friend's burden. *Nosei* also means "to lift up." Even when we can't help physically or financially, we can "uplift" and boost morale emotionally. There is always something we can do. We can *daven*. We can take on something on their behalf as a *zechus* for their *yeshuah*. We can take out the time to call them simply to let them know that they haven't been forgotten. When the *Ribono Shel Olam* sees that we think about one another and that we care about someone else's predicament, it directly impacts His sensitivity, *k'v'yachol*, to the situation at hand. Let us remember that the *pasuk* describes Hashem as our shadow ("*Hashem tzilcha al yad yeminecha*"[17]), and as such He mimics our behavior.

Esther was implored by Mordechai to go to King Achashverosh and plead for her people's survival. But it wasn't so simple. Anyone, even the queen, who went to the king without an invitation would be executed unless the king saw fit to extend his golden scepter.

Esther had not been invited. She took her life in her own hands by complying with Mordechai's request. She had but one request:

> *Lech knos es kol ha-Yehudim hanimtzaim b'Shushan* ***v'tzumu alai v'al tochlu v'al tishtu*** *sheloshes yamin lailah va-yom gam ani v'na'arosai atzum ken uv'chen avo el HaMelech asher lo k'das v'cha'asher avadti avadti* — *Go gather all of the Jews found in Shushan* **and fast for me and do not eat and drink** *for three days and nights, I and my maidservants will do the same. And so shall I go to the king unlawfully and whatever happens, happens.*

---

17 *Tehillim* 121:5.

The *pasuk* seems redundant. Why does it need to mention both "fast for me" and "don't eat and don't drink?" Isn't this precisely what fasting means?

Perhaps the *pasuk* is teaching us the very *yesod* of salvation as revealed by Esther. Her request that they fast is indeed outlined in the expression, "And they should not eat or drink." However, *v'tzumu alai*, fast **for me**, sends a different message: "Think of me, *daven* for me, join together with me, don't let me do this alone. Think about my plight. Feel my pain." *V'tzumu* can be interchanged with the word *v'sumu*, and place yourselves, *alai*, in my shoes. "If you do, then the *Ribono Shel Olam* will be forced, as it were, to do the same and we will all be saved. The combination of my *mesiras nefesh* on your behalf and yours on my behalf is a proven formula that brings salvation."

Indeed, it worked in Shushan and continues to work today.

Chapter 10

Recognition of the True Chashivus

Smear campaigns, slander, and the disgrace of that which is praiseworthy

Three sons left home, went out on their own, and prospered. Getting back together, they discussed the gifts they were able to give their elderly mother.

The first said, "I built a big house for our mother."

The second said, "I sent her a Mercedes with a driver."

The third smiled and said, "I've got you both beat. Remember how Mom enjoyed reading the Bible? And you know she can't see very well. I sent her a remarkable parrot that recites the entire Bible. It took twelve years to teach him. He's one of a kind. Mama just has to name the chapter and verse, and the parrot recites it."

Soon thereafter, Mom sent a letter to each son. "Milton,"

she wrote one son, "the house you built is so huge. I live in only one room, but I have to clean the whole house."

"Gerald," she wrote to another, "I am too old to travel. I stay most of the time at home, so I rarely use the Mercedes. And the driver is so rude!"

"Dearest Donald," she wrote to her third son, "you have the good sense to know what your mother likes. The chicken was delicious."

THE *Mesilas Yesharim* speaks about a type of blindness that is self-imposed. We begin to see things for what they are not and at the same time are oblivious to that which is obvious before our very eyes. I know when driving on the highway that exhaustion has taken over when the trees are waving at me. (It's even worse if I'm waving back at them!)

Sleep deprivation can do that. What about the gross distortions we are guilty of when we are wide awake? *Letzanus* has been defined as scoffing at and degrading something significant. Simply not appreciating something for its true value is a related form of *letzanus*, of which we are all guilty.

The quintessential *letz*, cynic, is Amalek. When all the inhabitants of Canaan trembled after having heard about the miracle of *kriyas Yam Suf* — the splitting of the Red Sea — Amalek wrote it off as *mikreh*, coincidence. When the hearts of other nations melted in fear and dread of this nation of G-d, Amalek even had the audacity to attack.

"*Reishis goyim Amalek v'achariso adei oved* — Amalek is the first of nations (to display such acrimonious behavior against Hashem and His people) and his end will be utter destruction."[18] Such a skeptic cannot possibly exist in a world of truth and will inevitably self-destruct at that time of *acharis hayamim* when all truth is revealed.

The *gematria*, numerical value, of the word Amalek is the same as *safek*, doubt: 240. Haman, the descendent of Agag, the king of Amalek,

18 Rav Yitzchak Hutner, *Pachad Yitzchak,* Purim 1.

dared to doubt the *chashivus* of Klal Yisrael, defaming them as a people who are "*mefuzar umeforad bein ha'amim* — spread out and removed from other nations":[19]

> *Their laws are different than [those of] regular people. They have many holidays when they can't go to work. They have to leave early on Fridays and on the eve of their festivals. If a fly was to fall into their wine, they would remove it and drink the rest, but if one of us were to merely touch their wine (even the king), they would throw out the entire contents. They're very strange people. They are of no value to us. They think they are better than us. Let's get rid of them.*

Like his ancestors and descendants, Haman was true to form in his hatred of Jews and vagrant display of smear and slander. The false testimony and libel campaign of Haman and all of his Amaleki cronies throughout history was paramount to their crusade of hate and murder.[20] But Hashem has a way of dealing with *eidim zomemim*, plotting witnesses, and indeed He did.

The celebration of Purim is a celebration of the removal of all doubts and the reinstating of *chashivus* to that which is truly important. It is the praising of the praiseworthy and the condemning of the despicable. In a sense, the Purim story was an enactment of the *din* of *eidim zomemim* in which we do to the false witnesses as they plotted to do to their victim ("*va'asisem lo ka'asher zamam la'asos l'achiv*"[21]). It is a fulfillment of the *pasuk* written in the same *parashah* of "*v'hitzdiku es hatzaddik v'hirshiu es harashah* — you shall reinstate the legitimacy of the falsely accused righteous one, and properly condemn the wicked (i.e., the false witnesses)."[22]

---

19 *Esther* 3:8.

20 Note that Hitler's success in persuading the masses was largely due to the establishment of a special bureau that used advertising and technology to portray Jews as vermin and parasites.

21 *Devarim* 19:19.

22 Ibid. 25:1.

Hashem orchestrated a precise reversal for those who dared to bear false witness against His people. Esther replaced Vashti, Mordechai replaced Haman, mourning turned into celebration, and fasting into feasting. Strangely enough, the impudent disgrace of using the vessels of the Beis HaMikdash as part of the *fleish*-fest of Achashverosh's gastronomic display of self-indulgent delight led to the rebuilding of the Beis HaMikdash by virtue of the dictates of the very son of Achashverosh and Esther, Daryavesh, the bringing of *korbanos*, and a return to sincere dedication to Hashem. The unwarranted defamation was replaced with: "*V'rabim me-amei ha'aretz misYahadim ki nafal pachad Mordechai aleihem* — And many of the Gentiles converted to Judaism as the fear of Mordechai fell upon them."[23] Justice was served. The truth emerged. All doubt fell away as the glory of Hashem was revealed.

May we celebrate many more such reversals, and may the world become enlightened by the truth of the *chashivus* of the Almighty and his people, *b'vias haMashiach, bimheirah b'yameinu, Amen*!

23 *Esther* 8:17.

CHAPTER 11

TALKING DOGS

THE BRAZENNESS OF AMALEK VS. THE HUMILITY OF KLAL YISRAEL

A man sees a sign in front of a house: "Talking Dog for Sale." He rings the bell and the owner tells him that the dog is in the backyard. He goes into the backyard and sees a black mutt just sitting there.

"You talk?" he asks.

"Yep," the mutt replies.

"So, what's your story?"

The mutt looks up and says, "Well, I discovered this gift pretty young and I wanted to help the government, so I told the CIA about my gift, and in no time they had me jetting from country to country, sitting in rooms with spies and world leaders, because no one figured a dog would be eavesdropping.

"I was one of their most valuable spies eight years running. But, the jetting around really tired me out, and I knew I wasn't getting any younger, and so I wanted to settle down.

"I signed up for a job at the airport to do some undercover security work, mostly wandering near suspicious characters

and listening in. I uncovered some incredible dealings there and was awarded a batch of medals.

"I then had a wife, a mess of puppies, and now I'm just retired."

The man is amazed. He goes back in and asks the owner what he wants for the dog.

The owner says, "Give me five dollars."

The guy says, "Five dollars? That's all? This dog is amazing. He just told me about his illustrious career and life's accomplishments! Why on earth are you selling him so cheap?"

"Oh! He's such a liar," the owner replies. "He didn't do any of those things."

HAMAN was proud to announce that only he had been invited by Queen Esther to join her and Achashverosh at a private feast. He was delighted with all his life's accomplishments, the fortune he had amassed, and the power he wielded. He was the prototypical *hedyot kofetz b'rosh* — the base person who jumps forward to respond first in spite of his lower position. Despite his lowly position as the most insignificant of the king's advisors, Haman was the first to suggest a solution in regard to Vashti's recalcitrant behavior and brazenly recommend the execution of the queen. Indeed, he acted very much like a dog running ahead of his master as if to take the lead, but who — at the end of the day — is merely an impudent dog. Not only did he not know his place, but like so many ambitious megalomaniacs he would also never be satisfied until everyone in the kingdom bowed down to him. Mordechai's refusal to capitulate infuriated him, and Haman could not rest until he orchestrated a plan that included the mass annihilation of Mordechai and his people. In the end, he reaped nothing from his attainments and died in humiliation and indignity, hanged together with his ten sons. Much like his cohorts in recent history (e.g., Hitler, Sadaam, Quadafi, and Bin Laden), Haman met a miserable death of disgrace and ignominy, valueless and inconsequential, having sacrificed eternity for futility.

It is precisely this lesson that we celebrate on Purim: the victory of unpretentiousness over self-importance, of humility over brazenness, of modesty over arrogance. The *pasuk* in *Mishlei* teaches: "*Ul'anavim yiten chen* — to the humble He gives charm."[24] Esther, according to one opinion in the Gemara was not very attractive (as implied in her name Hadassah, which connotes that she was of a green complexion like the color of a myrtle branch, i.e., not a complimentary appellation), but she was blessed with an unusual charm and charisma. Everyone was drawn to her. Achashverosh selected her over hundreds of others. The masses thought that she was their compatriot and embraced her. She was blessed with a *chut shel chesed* — a strand of graciousness from above, deserving as she was, because of her modest nature and because she humbled herself before Hashem.

Vashti, on the other hand, was the epitome of licentious pretentiousness, willing to come before the king and his inebriated constituency in a state of absolute immodesty. This "noble" descendent of royalty so promiscuous and wanton was replaced with an Esther HaMalkah, a true queen, a devoted princess of the *mamleches kohanim v'goy kadosh*.

Everyone bowed to the wicked Haman. All, that is, except Mordechai, as it says: "*U'Mordechai lo yichra v'lo yishtachaveh*."[25] But it wasn't a pompousness that prevented him from succumbing to the order of the king. It was his humility before the King of all kings. The double expression, "He would not bend and would not bow," is indicative of Mordechai's position. He would not bend — he would not cave in or yield to the arrogance and defiance of a Haman. Like other *rabbanim* in the Holocaust, beaten to a pulp by their merciless Nazi tormentors, who somehow picked themselves up off the ground and stood up tall so as not to yield to the Nazi attempt to disgrace Hashem and His people, Mordechai refused to relinquish to the Amaleki and his cohort Achashverosh, the *kelavim*, dogs, that surrounded him.[26]

---

24 *Mishlei* 3:34.

25 *Esther* 3:2.

26 As in the verse: "*Ki sevavuni kelavim adas mereim hikifuni* — For dogs surrounded me, evildoers encircled me," found in *Tehillim* 22:17, the chapter of *Ayelet Hashachar* that alludes to Purim.

Rabbi Yisrael Meir Lau, *shlit"a*, in his classic book *Out of the Depths*, writes the following about what he witnessed as a five-year-old during a pitiless beating of his very own father, the Rav of Piortkow:

> *The captain of the Piortkow Gestapo approached my father, a deadly look in his eye. He stopped and, pulling out his maikeh, a rubber club about three-feet long, began to beat my father on the back with all his might. When the first blow struck my father from behind, the surprise and force of it made him stagger. His body bent forward as if he was about to topple over. And then, in a fraction of a second, he straightened up to his full height, stepped back, and returned to the place where he had been standing. There, he stood erect, making a supreme effort to hide his physical pain as well as his intense humiliation. I could see father mustering up all of his strength to keep his balance and avoid collapsing at the German officer's feet. Father knew that if he fell, the spirit of the entire town would break, and he was trying desperately to prevent that.*

Such was the courage of many a humble servant of Hashem who, like Esther and Mordechai, were willing to risk their lives for the sake of *kavod Shamayim*. May we merit the day when all such *mesiras nefesh* is met with miracles from Above as Klal Yisrael experienced years ago in Shushan!

Chapter 12

Mirrors of the Soul

Facing the Reality of the Abstract and the Concrete

Recently divorced, a middle-aged woman moved back to her hometown hoping to start over again. A few weeks later, while making a dentist appointment, she was surprised to see that she recognized the dentist's name as the same as a nice-looking wholesome boy who attended her high school twenty-five years before. However, upon walking into the dentist's office, she quickly realized he must be someone else. He was bald, had a considerable beer belly, and looked a lot older than she. Just to be sure, though, on her way out she asked him if he went to the high school that she had attended.

"Yes," he responded, "I graduated in 1987."

"Oh my gosh," she said excitedly, "you were in my class!"

"Really," he said. "That's interesting. What class did you teach?"

WE are often guilty of shifting the blame or imposing our views on others. We most certainly allow our partisanship to impact our impressions, and we are likely to distort the reality in the process unless we are brutally honest. The image we see in the mirror is not necessarily what others see. Our sense of worth, for better or for worse, is a reflection of what quite possibly could border on being an aberration or delusion. I distinctly remember my *rebbi*, Harav Shlomo Freifeld, *zt"l*, telling a *talmid* who was deliberating about his lack of attraction to a *shidduch* he was in the midst of: "Listen, my friend. You're not exactly Prince Charming yourself!" He wasn't trying to insult the young man (Rabbi Freifeld was a tremendous builder of character), and he wasn't denying the importance of attraction in a *shidduch*. He was simply reshaping the balance in order to shift this young man back to reality about himself and his expectations. It's so easy to get lost and twist that equilibrium into a slight delusion of grandeur or a significant "selling oneself short." It works both ways, with the latter resulting in a loss of perspective and an incredible forfeiture of kinetic energy and the potential of talent untapped.

Purim is all about reversal. It is all about the reality of the abstract and the illusion of the tangible. In a general sense, the Purim story proclaims the continuous presence of Hashem's *hashgachah* through what seemed to be removed and hidden. On a personal level, it is a day of *teshuvah* and introspection. It is the counterpart of Yom Kippur (*Yom Kippurim* — a day like Purim), but very different from Yom Kippur. Unlike Yom Kippur, when we try to imitate angels through the five *inuyim*, afflictions, on Purim we engage the phenomenon of "*nichnas yayin yotzei sod* — the wine enters and the secrets are revealed," in order to remove all barriers in our declaration of oneness with Hashem. The goal is the same but the approach is different — to the extreme. With an emphasis on the physical, i.e., on feasting and drinking, we loosen the inhibitions and release the spiritual to soar together with a *guf*, physical body, that has become a willing partner rather than an earthly antagonist. Purim is the metamorphosis of the *guf* as a spiritual entity — a reversal of massive proportions and eternal ramifications. It is a day when we face the reality that the *neshamah* can, in fact, influence the *guf* and reign over it with majesty and splendor.

Come and see the *nichnas-yayin-yatza-sod Yid* from whom Torah, *ahavas Hashem*, and *ahavas habrios* pours forth. Unlike other inebriated persons, whose behavior patterns quickly decline to folly and to that of a goofball, this *Yid*'s self-image undergoes a transformation to a *guf* that has been influenced by its *neshamah* counterpart, and together the *sod* emanates, the truth is revealed, the abstract surfaces, and the physical being becomes a mere mirror of the soul.

Chapter 13

To the Bitter End

Man's worst fate — the loss of bechirah

An atheist was taking a walk through the woods, admiring all that the "accident of evolution" had created. "What beautiful animals!" he said to himself.

As he walked alongside the river, he heard a rustling in the bushes behind him. He turned to look. He saw a seven-foot grizzly bear charging toward him. He ran as fast as he could up the path. He looked over his shoulder and saw that the bear was closing in. He ran even faster, so scared that tears were coming to his eyes. Looking over his shoulder again, he saw that the bear was even closer. His heart was pumping frantically and he tried to run even faster. He tripped and fell on the ground.

He rolled over to pick himself up, but he saw the bear, right on top of him, reaching for him with his left paw and raising his right paw to strike.

At that instant the atheist cried out, without thinking, "Oh my G-d!"

Time stopped. The bear froze. The forest was silent. Even the river stopped moving.

As a bright light shone upon the man, a voice came out of the sky, "You deny my existence for all of these years, teach others I don't exist, and even credit creation to a cosmic accident. Do you expect me to help you out of this predicament? Am I to now count you as a believer?"

The atheist looked directly into the light and answered, "To be perfectly honest, it would be hypocritical for me to proclaim myself as a believer after all these years; but, perhaps, you could spare my life by making the bear a believer in Your laws."

"Very well," said the voice. "I'll try."

The light went out. The river ran again. The sounds of the forest resumed.

And then the bear dropped his right paw, brought both paws together, bowed his head and spoke:

"Lord, for this food which I am about to receive, I am truly thankful."

DID you ever wonder what Haman was thinking as he was about to be hanged on the very gallows he prepared for Mordechai? Was he remorseful? Did he recognize the *yad Hashem*? Did he repent or did he remain steadfast in his corruption to his very last moment?

Chazal tell us that *reshaim* are well aware of the path they have chosen and to where it will lead them, and nonetheless they continue down that path to the bitter end. Their indifference to the reality they face is, in a sense, the most severe punishment possible, for is there a worse fate in life than to lose one's *bechirah*, freedom of choice? It is precisely that *bechirah* and the difficult challenges it brings with it that afford us the auspicious opportunity to overcome and achieve eternity. It is that *bechirah* that allows us to return in *teshuvah sheleimah*. When Hashem hardened the heart of Pharaoh, it was because he had reached a level of malevolence that made him no longer worthy of the opportunity to return.

In the news today, there are countless reports of murderers, rapists, child abusers, tyrants, predators, and other horrific individuals who have destroyed the lives of others and their families in cold blood, literally or emotionally, and show no remorse or shame for their malicious behavior.

It gets worse. In certain Middle Eastern countries, terrorists who have killed innocent men, women, and children are treated as champions, paraded around as heroes on the very streets that are named in their honor. The dictum of Chazal that says: "*B'derech she'adam rotzeh lelech bo molichin oso* — According to the path a man has chosen to follow is he led upon,"[27] certainly applies to *reshaim* in the negative sense. That choice can prove to be their undoing, and perhaps their very last *bechirah*.

In the world in which we live, it is far too easy to become entrenched in a *yetzer hara* that leaves us much too close to a place of no return. At times, we may wonder if we have any *bechirah* left, or if we have cast away our opportunity to climb out of our self-imposed incarceration. On Purim, it is important to recognize that reversal is in the air and return is quite feasible.

We may have erred or let a *ta'avah*, desire, get the best of us or even take hold of our behavior in the most controlling fashion. Nonetheless, we are not evil. We have not come close to the *madreigah* of a Haman, Hitler, Saddam Hussein, or Quadafi. We are not Pharaoh. We still have *bechirah*, and we can thus do *teshuvah* and merit the *segulah*, the propitious opportunity, of "*asher yishletu haYehudim heimah b'soneihem* — that the Jews will rule over their enemies," the greatest enemy being the *yetzer hara*. Let us take full advantage.

---

27 *Makkos* 10b.

Chapter 14

Everyone Should Enjoy Purim

Getting drunk from Purim itself

It has been said in jest that the reason why four pesukim in Megillas Esther are read to the sad tune of Eichah (Lamentations) is so that the Litvishe Jews (the "Misnagdim") should enjoy Purim as well!

If so, the question is asked, why don't they read the entire Megillah to the somber tune of Eichah if that's what makes them happy?

The rejoining answer is: absolutely not! Tzu fil hollilus — that would be too much frivolity!

IT is indeed unfortunate that for some, Purim has become a day of buffoonery and clowning in a wild display of irresponsible inebriation. This "Mardi Gras" approach to a day that is the counterpart of Yom Kippur makes such behavior not only distasteful but displays a pitifully superficial understanding the holiness of the day. The true *simchah* of Purim, as well as its auspicious opportunity for growth in a short twenty-four-hour period of time, demands that we reassess our outlook of this special day.

The obvious question is: since when is consuming large measures of alcohol a Jewish concept, let alone a mitzvah?

Yet, Chazal say that a person is obligated to become intoxicated on Purim until he can no longer discern between "Cursed be Haman" and "Blessed be Mordechai."[28] Could it be that our Sages are instructing us to simply get "wasted out of our minds" one day a year in a wild and brainless celebration that leaves its victims mopping up floors and cleaning their carpets?

Of course not. A closer examination of the terminology of Chazal's words is in order.

In reference to Chazal's uncharacteristic directive to imbibe, i.e., "to sweeten through Purim" (as opposed to "becoming drunk with wine," [*Rashi*]), as well as the measure of becoming oblivious to the distinction between the despised Haman and the revered Mordechai which begs for interpretation, would it not have been more correct to write *l'shikurei b'chamrah b'Purya*, that a person is obligated to become intoxicated by drinking wine on Purim, rather than the vague *l'vesumei b'Purya*, to sweeten through Purim? In addition, isn't it a basic tenet of *hashkafah* for a Jew to clearly recognize the differences between the righteous man and the wicked one at all times and seasons, and never to equate them?

The well-known declaration of Chazal that we sing so gleefully, "*Mishenichnas Adar marbim b'simchah* — When Adar is ushered in we increase in joy," is actually only part of the quote. The Gemara in *Taanis* says: "*K'shem she'mishenichnas Av mam'itin b'simchah, kach mishenichnas Adar marbim b'simchah* — Just as one diminishes his joy with the ushering in of the month of Av, so shall he increase his joy as he ushers in the month of Adar."[29] For some reason, Chazal stress a correlation between the joy of Adar and the mourning of Av. The use of the words *k'shem*, just as, and *kach*, so too, make this abundantly clear. Another indication of the curious relationship between mourning and rejoicing is the custom to read four *pesukim* in *Megillas Esther* to the minor diatonic scale

28 *Megillah* 7b.

29 *Ta'anis* 29a.

of the *trop* of *Eichah*, and the fact that it is so easily blended into the *megillah* reading by the *baal koreh* from the major scale of the *trop* of *Esther*. What is this all about?

Again, the relationship between rejoicing and mourning is underscored in the prayer immediately following the *tekiyos* before *Mussaf* on Rosh Hashanah. There we say: "*B'shimcha yigilun kol hayom u'b'tzidkascha yarumu* — In Your name, Hashem, they shall rejoice the entire day (and every day), and in Your righteousness they shall exalt You."[30] The *sefarim haKedoshim* point out that, peculiarly, the beginning letters of the words "*b'shimcha yigilun kol hayom*" spell the word *bechiyah*, crying.[31]

Apparently, when a Jew focuses on Hashem's name each and every day, no matter the events of that day, then his crying is on par with his rejoicing. The cry of a Jew is never the cry of discouragement and despair; it is one of hope and trust in the name of Hashem. His tears are inevitably tears of joy, as his closeness with his Creator is enhanced by virtue of his plight. This enigma is further reconciled by our firm belief that the *Ribono Shel Olam* is indeed entirely good, and that His will is only to do good, even though at times that good is concealed from us. The halachah of "*k'shem shemevarchim al ha-tov kach mevarchim al hara* — just as we bless [Hashem] for the good, so we must bless [Him] for the bad,"[32] is a manifestation of our steadfast conviction that whatever Hashem does is for the good. To the true believer, there is nothing that transpires during the course of his life that is not part of the master plan of the Master Planner to benefit him in some way.

Even so, it is rare that we are privileged to see the whole picture that unequivocally reveals the unraveling of the mystery and the revelation of Hashem's glory in its wake.

Purim is one of those rare occasions. The amazing reversal of events allowed all of Klal Yisrael to witness the good in the guise of bad in full exposure. The halachah of *k'shem shemevarchim al ha-tov kach mevarchim*

---

30 *Tehillim* 89:17.

31 Rabbi Yaakov Meir Schechter, *Leket Amarim*.

32 *Berachos* 54a.

al hara became a simple matter, as Klal Yisrael basked in the glory of having seen the whole picture. We can well understand why the joy of Adar is part and parcel of the mourning of Av, as that joy is not limited to the appreciation of the good but is heightened by the appreciation of the bad, as well, as part of the same symphony. The *k'shem she'mishenichnas Av mam'itin b'simchah kach mishenichnas Adar marbim b'simchah* relationship is identical to the *k'sheim shemevarchim al ha-tov kach mevarchim al hara* relationship of good and bad. It is all good in the complete picture.

Now it all makes sense. It's not the irresponsible drinking of wine that should intoxicate us as much as Purim itself and the revelation of G-d being ever-present in the natural world — that indeed *yesh Hashem b'kirbenu* — Hashem is in our midst! A person is obligated *l'vesumei*, to sweeten, i.e., to find the sweetness in what appears to be a harsh decree, to see the good in the bad, *b'Purya*, through the amazing revelation of Purim until the point where he recognizes that even the wickedness of Haman is the equivalent of the good of Mordechai in the bigger and broader picture.

A story to illustrate the point: It was Erev Rosh Chodesh Adar 5768 toward evening, as the new month of Adar Sheni was about to begin. A dear friend and I were on our way to Har Nof in Yerushalayim. We had just made a right turn from Sderot Herzl and were about to pass Yeshivat Merkaz Harav. Then we saw the police, the street roped off, people running frantically, and we heard the screams, and then the shots ringing out that mercilessly took the lives of the eight *kedoshim, Hy"d*. Even after we were whisked away from the scene, we remained frozen in shock from what we had just witnessed. That night, I was scheduled to speak at Yeshivas Ner Yaakov at a gathering to celebrate Rosh Chodesh Adar and the feeling of euphoria that it usually generates. This year, however, it would be different. We all sat there, stunned by the events of the evening, trying desperately to reconcile how such a feeling of mourning could coexist with a call to increase in joy.

Then it came together. The greatest joy possible is to feel the presence of the *Ribono Shel Olam* — to feel close to Him; to recognize how small we are and how great He is, to understand how desperately we are dependent on Him and how incapable we are without His constant infusion of life and vitality, to perceive that our knowledge is so limited and that we therefore subjugate ourselves to His mastery of the world and all that transpires — for Hashem sees and knows the whole picture. With tears in our eyes we rejoiced in the knowledge that someday we will merit to see the good even in such a calamity, and we will recognize deeply in our hearts that "Hashem is the G-d in the heavens above and in the earth below; there is none other."[33]

33 *Devarim* 4:39.

Chapter 15

Who's a Jew?

Hakaras Ha-tov — the Trademark of a Jew

An elderly Jewish woman was flying back from Florida to New York when she turned to the gentleman seated next to her and asked, "Excuse me, but are you Jewish?"

"No, ma'am," he answered politely. "I'm not Jewish."

A few minutes later, the woman turned to the man again and asked, "You're sure you're not Jewish?"

With great patience, he answered once again, "No ma'am, I'm really not Jewish!"

Ten minutes later, the persistent old woman asked a third time, "Are you positive you're not Jewish?"

"Yes, ma'am, I'm positive that I'm not Jewish!" the seatmate answered emphatically.

Five minutes later, she said again, "Please tell me the truth! Are you Jewish?"

Losing his patience, this time the man changed his tune. "Okay, ma'am, I give in. You win! Yes! I am Jewish!"

"That's funny," the woman responded. "You don't look Jewish!"

THE essence of a *Yid* is measured by the degree to which he shows gratitude and appreciation for all that he receives in life. One "looks Jewish" when he lives up to his name *Yehudi*, which stems from the root word of *hoda'ah*, thanksgiving. The name our matriarch Leah gave her son Yehudah was based upon her *hakaras ha-tov*, appreciation, that she had been given a fourth son, proving that she had merited more than her one-fourth portion in Klal Yisrael. "*Ha-pa'am odeh es Hashem* — Now I will thank Hashem," she said as she named her son Yehudah.[34]

Such has been the legacy of this nation of *Yehudim*, Jews, for a Jew always believes that he has received more than his portion and is eternally grateful for it. Jewishness is not a manifestation of any physical attribute (with all due respect to noses!). It is rather a manifestation of one's ability to recognize the good one has been given and to trace everything back to the One Source Who gave it all to him: Hashem.

The *pasuk* in *Mishlei* says: "*Ish l'fi mehalalo* — Each man according to his praise."[35] There are many explanations of this phrase:

- Rabbeinu Yonah says that it means that man is defined according to what he praises.
- Others say it means that man is defined by the manner in which others praise him.
- Perhaps the simplest yet most essential explanation is that the true essence of a man can be measured according to the degree in which he praises and expresses appreciation. This is the true measure of a member of the nation called *Yehudim*.

"*LaYehudim haisah orah v'simchah v'sason v'yekar* — To the Jews there was light, happiness, joy, and honor."[36] The Gemara in *Megillah* elucidates that *orah* is referring to Torah, *simchah* to Yom Tov, *sason* to

---

34 *Bereishis* 29:35.

35 Ibid. 27:21.

36 *Esther* 8:16.

bris milah, and *yekar* to *tefillin*.[37] Haman's decrees had precluded the performance of these mitzvos that were now restored to Klal Yisrael.

Without a doubt, the removal of Haman and the newly found excitement about Torah and mitzvos was a product of a keen understanding and appreciation for each of the mitzvos and a deep *hakaras ha-tov* for the privilege of serving Hashem. Perhaps this is why the *pasuk* specifically chooses to identify the Jews as *Yehudim*, as it was this propensity toward *hoda'ah* — which has always been the trademark of a Jew — that led them to the appreciation of these mitzvos. Indeed, at this time they were truly Jews living up to their name as the quintessential *makirei tov*, grateful people.

Rav Elazar Menachem Shach, *zt"l*, once insisted on traveling to a town near Haifa to attend a funeral despite his frailty, his advanced age, and the inclement weather. He was acoompanied by his grandson who was even more bewildered at his *zeide*'s insistence to travel when he realized that it was the funeral of an unknown elderly woman and that it was attended by barely a *minyan* of other men. As they returned to the taxi from the burial, Rav Shach stood in the rain for a few minutes, lost in his thoughts. Upon entering the taxi, he explained that as a *bachur* in yeshiva in Lithuania some seventy years earlier, due to a lack of other accommodations he was forced to sleep on a bench in a cold *beis medrash*. The cold bothered him more and more to the point where he began to have thoughts of leaving the yeshiva. The time arrived when he decided that he could no longer endure the cold that crept into his bones and that he would leave the next morning.

Miraculously, that very night a different solution presented itself. A man who had been a seller of quilts had passed away and his young widow decided to donate his leftover stock to various yeshivos. The young Rav Shach was one of the fortunate recipients of her kindness. Finally having had a warm night's sleep, he felt refreshed and rejuvenated in spirit and decided to remain in yeshiva.

---

37 *Megillah* 16b.

Rav Shach never forgot the *chesed* of this woman, who later settled in Eretz Yisrael. Even though it was some seven decades later, upon learning of her passing Rav Shach would not allow anything to stop him from paying his last respects. And for the few minutes before entering the taxi, he stood out in the rain so that he could feel the chill in his bones that he had felt years before in the cold *beis medrash* and thus properly express his *hakaras ha-tov* one last time to the *nifteres*. Such was the never-ending *hakaras ha-tov* of the *gadol hador* who taught his generation what it means to "look like a Jew."

CHAPTER 16

RECOGNIZING THE GOOD

HA'ARACHAS HA-TOV — PROPER APPRECIATION OF THE GOOD BY TRACING ITS SOURCE

Fred and Bill were working at the sawmill when Bill accidentally sawed his arm off. Fred quickly scooped up the detached arm, placed it in a plastic bag, and promptly rushed his friend to the hospital.

The next day, upon visiting the hospital, Fred was shocked to find Bill in rehab playing tennis.

"Wow!" said Fred. "The wonders of modern science!"

On his first day back at work, Bill had another mishap, this time sawing off his leg. Reacting with alacrity, Fred carefully placed the severed leg in a plastic bag and rushed Bill to the hospital.

The next day at the hospital, Fred was astounded to find Bill outside playing football. "Wow! The wonders of modern medicine," he said.

The two were soon back at work together, when this time it was Fred who leaned in too far, and accidentally chopped off his head. Bill, eager to repay his friend's favors, wasted no time as he carefully placed the detached head into a plastic bag and rushed Fred to the hospital.

The next day Bill came to the hospital to see how Fred was doing, but to his dismay, his friend was nowhere to be found. "Where's Fred?" he asked the nurse.

"It's very sad," the nurse responded. "We might have saved him, but some fool put his head in a plastic bag and suffocated him to death!"

HOW difficult it is, at times, to repay a favor. It is an even greater challenge to recognize all the good that is done for us and to trace its source so that proper appreciation can be expressed. The familiar expression of *hakaras ha-tov*, recognition of the good, as opposed to *ha'arachas ha-tov*, appreciation of the good, implies a need to trace back and uncover all that may have contributed to the benefit, pleasure, or relief of which we have been the fortunate recipients.

The *Midrash Rabbah* makes this point abundantly clear. When Moshe helped the daughters of Yisro, they went home and reported to their father: "*Ish Mitzri hitzilanu* — An Egyptian man saved us [from the hands of the predacious shepherds]."[38] The typical understanding of "*Ish Mitzri*" is that it refers to Moshe Rabbeinu, who had fled to Midyan from Mitzrayim.

The Midrash, however, offers a different explanation, comparing Moshe to a man who was bitten by a snake and then ran to the closest body of water to immerse his wound and neutralize the venom. Once upon the river, the man was startled by the desperate cries of a child gasping for air about to drown. Immediately, the man jumped into the water and saved the child's life. After being revived, the child emotionally expressed his appreciation to his savior. "Thank you so much! If not for you, I would have drowned!"

---

38 *Shemos* 2:19.

"Don't thank me," the man replied. "Thank the snake that bit me. For were it not for that snake, I would have never run to the river!"

Similarly, the *Ish Mitzri* referred to in the *pasuk* is not Moshe Rabbeinu but rather the Egyptian that Moshe slew in Mitzrayim. It was that Egyptian's death that forced Moshe to flee to Midyan, affording him the opportunity to save the daughters of Yisro. "Don't thank me," Moshe said to Yisro's daughters. "Thank that native Egyptian, for were it not for my encounter with him, I would have never come to Midyan." This consummate *hakaras ha-tov*, when reported to Yisro, made an indelible impression upon him and certainly contributed to his ultimate embrace of Judaism.

The Mishnah in *Avos* teaches: "Whoever repeats a statement in the name of its originator brings redemption to the world."[39] Just as Queen Esther ultimately brought about a redemption for the Jewish people by reporting in Mordechai's name the plot of Bigsan and Seresh to assassinate the king, so too does anyone who repeats a statement in the name of its originator bring redemption to the world. This is because *geulah*, redemption, by definition means tracing everything in existence back to the One Source, Hashem. The Maharal explains that the act of repeating a statement in the name of its originator — a small gesture of *hakaras ha-tov* — is actually an act of redemption, because through doing so one is seeking out the origin of his benefit. Indeed, the ultimate redemption will come when all of mankind will see the *Ribono Shel Olam* as the Source of everything and will finally trace all that exists in the world to Him.

As stated, it is not a simple matter to uncover the source of all the good we receive and to have a complete *hakaras ha-tov* for the blessings in our life, but it is certainly worthwhile for us to try to do so. For when we accustom ourselves to this approach to life, we will engage in small but significant acts of redemption that will ultimately bring about the Final Redemption, speedily and in our days, *Amen*.

LaYehudim haisah orah v'simchah v'sason v'yekar, ken tihye lanu!

---

39 *Avos* 6:6.

Part 2: Chanukah

A Time to Reveal

Chapter 1

The Perpetuation of the Inexplicable

We will never forget Har Sinai.

While on a car trip, an old couple stopped at a roadside restaurant for lunch. The old woman unfortunately left her glasses on the table but didn't realize they were missing until they were back on the highway.

By then, they had to travel quite a distance before they could find a place to turn around. The old man was quite upset about his wife's forgetfulness and fussed and complained all the way back to the restaurant.

When they finally arrived, as the old woman got out of the car to retrieve her glasses, the old man said, "While you're in there, you may as well get my hat and the credit card too."

IN the *Al Hanisim* prayer, the major objective of the Yevanim is described succinctly as "*l'hashkicham Torasecha* — to make them (the Jews) forget Your Torah." Indeed, they had a precise plan how to accomplish their goal, as stated in the following phrase: "*Ul'ha'aviram mei-chukei retzonecha* — And to cause them to transgress the *chukim* of Your will."

Chok refers to an incomprehensible law that is difficult (if not impossible) to rationalize intellectually. *Parah adumah*, *hilchos niddah*, and *tefillin* are just a few examples of classic *chukim* that comprise a significant part of *taryag mitzvos*. These Yevanim, who idolized the intellect of man, would shudder at the thought of a people willing to observe in an unquestioning manner that which they did not understand intellectually. It was contrary to all that they idealized. By imposing certain *gezeros* and by tantalizing the *Yidden* with an alternative to Torah that was intellectually stimulating, the *shich'chas haTorah* process began. The icing on the cake was to once and for all ensure the eradication of *Yiddishkeit* by removing blind observance of the inexplicable and the *bittul* of the self to a Higher Authority. The *chukim* had to go. They understood such observance was the lifeblood of *ehrliche Yidden*. The Greeks had no tolerance for such dogma. It was incongruent to their creed of life, which was the worship of the *seichel*, man's intellect.

Truth be told, though, all mitzvos, even the most rational, are to be approached as if they were *chukim* and performed simply because they are the decree of the King of all kings, *Melech Malchei HaMelachim HaKadosh Baruch Hu*. An *ehrliche* Jew keeps every mitzvah because it is the *ratzon Hashem* and not because it appeals to his passions, intellect, or emotions.

The Mishnah in *Berachos* states: "*Ha'omer al kan tzipur 'yagiu rachamecha' meshaskin oso* — if one says (in praise of Hashem), 'Your mercy is so great that it even reaches out to the bird's nest (in that You commanded the mitzvah of *shiluach haken,* to send away the mother bird before snatching the young fledglings or taking the eggs),' we silence him."[40] The Gemara explains that in making such a statement, one is declaring Hashem's mitzvos are to be acclaimed because they exhibit compassion and thereby appeal to our emotions and common sense, when in fact they are to be observed simply because they are the decree of the King.

The point is unequivocal. Every mitzvah is to be observed as if it was a *chok*. This explains the reason the Torah introduced the *parashah*

---

40 *Berachos* 33b.

of *parah adumah*, the archetypical *chok*, with the words "*zos chukas ha-Torah* — these are the laws of the Torah,"[41] and not with an introduction to the discussion at hand, namely the red heifer. It should have written "*zos chukas haparah* — these are the laws of the cow," which would have been specific to the instruction that follows, rather than the generic expression "these are the *chukim* of the Torah."

Perhaps we can suggest that the *pasuk* wanted to emphasize the very point of the Gemara above. Every mitzvah should be approached as if it was a *chok* — even the most *seicheldik*, compassionate, and humanistic ones. They are all the decrees of the King, and we are His loyal servants, privileged and thrilled to do His bidding.

Let the Yevanim of yesteryear and of today try all they want to appeal to mankind to succumb to the temptation to believe in his intellect even to the point of heresy. We will not budge from the commitment we made at Har Sinai, where our enthusiastic "*na'aseh v'nishmah* — we will do [even before we know the details]" was predicated on a mountain lifted above our heads threatening to bury us alive — not because we needed to be forced, but because we accepted with great love and yearning that "*retzonenu liheyos kefufim* — it is our pure desire to be forced," where the understanding of the privilege to be an *eved Hashem* reigned supreme.[42] We shall never forget how we accepted the Torah and will never be persuaded to abandon our acceptance of the entire Torah in the realm of the decree of the King of all kings!

---

41 *Bamidbar* 19:2.

42 *Ohr Gedalyahu*, Shavuos 3, pg. 163.

CHAPTER 2

CHANUKAH GIFTS

THE GREAT GIFT OF NISIM B'DERECH HA-TEVA

At the last moment, Marty remembered to put on one of the two neckties his mother had given him as a Chanukah gift the night before at the family Chanukah party.

"Thank G-d I remembered," he thought as he approached the door of his parents' home where he had been invited for Shabbos. Opening the door, Marty's mother took one look at the tie he was wearing and said, "What's wrong? You didn't like the other one?"

THE *Ribono Shel Olam*, in His interminable graciousness, bestowed upon Klal Yisrael two distinct miracles for which we celebrate the Yom Tov of Chanukah. There was the amazing miracle of the military victory, in which just a small group of Chashmona'im won over the massive armies of Antiochus, and there was the well-known miracle of the single flask of oil that burned in the menorah for eight days. Although the military victory is referred to as a *nes b'derech ha-teva*, a miracle disguised in the facade of nature, and the oil is considered a *nes shelo b'derech ha-teva*, an unnatural occurrence, clearly both are miracles from Hashem. This is just like Rabbi Chanina Ben Dosa famously said to his forlorn daughter who had inadvertently used vinegar instead of oil for the Shabbos lights: "Do not worry, my dear daughter! He Who instructed oil to burn will instruct vinegar to burn as well."[43] Everything is a miracle. Although oil burning is a "regular" occurrence, one that is in accordance with the laws of nature, it is still no less a miracle than the unlikely combustion of vinegar. Engulfed as we are in this well-disguised *olam ha-teva*, world of nature, we are all too easily fooled, and we fail to recognize the miracles that abound.

One of the classic answers to the well-known question of the Beis Yosef as to why we celebrate eight days of Chanukah when the Jews, in fact, had enough oil for one night, lies in the dual miracles of Chanukah. The first day commemorates the miracle of the war, and the remaining seven days commemorate the miracle of the oil. Both miracles were equally magnificent; both were amazing gifts from above.

The Gemara asks the question, "*Mai Chanukah* — What is Chanukah?"[44] Rashi explains the Gemara's question more pointedly, saying that the question is examining the primary motivation for the establishment of the Yom Tov of Chanukah. "*Al eizeh nes kavuha* — Due to which of the two miracles did the Sages establish this Yom Tov?" Was it the miracle of the war or the miracle of the oil? Was it the *nes b'derech ha-teva* — the *nes nistar* — hidden miracle, or was it the *nes shelo b'derech ha-teva* — the *nes niglah* — revealed miracle?

The Gemara proceeds to quote a *beraisah* that discusses the events of the twenty-fifth of Kislev and emphasizes the miracle of the oil. Clearly, the Gemara is convinced that the Sages would never have established the Yom Tov of Chanukah had it not been for the *nes shelo b'derech ha-teva*. Yet in the *Al Hanisim* that we insert in our prayers on Chanukah, the emphasis is predominantly on the miracle of the war, which we won against all odds. In fact, the *nes* of the oil is only mentioned briefly, almost as if it were an afterthought! This becomes even more confusing when one

---

43 *Ta'anis* 25a.

44 *Shabbos* 21b.

considers that Rav Chaim Shmulevitz, *zt"l*, comments that without a doubt the miracle of the war and the relief it provided for an outnumbered and endangered Klal Yisrael clearly outshines the miracle of the oil![45] So again we ask: which was the primary miracle? Which was the one for which Chanukah was established as a Yom Tov?

It may very well be that the primary miracle of the Yom Tov of Chanukah was the miraculous victory on the battlefield, as emphasized in the *Al Hanisim*, while the miracle of the oil, the "unnatural occurrence," was performed in order to serve as a Divine message to the Sages to establish these days as a Yom Tov, as emphasized in the Gemara. It was a communication from Above that indeed the miracle of the war, the *nes b'derech ha-teva*, is as much of a miracle as the miracle of the oil, the *nes shelo b'derech ha-teva*.

The message of Chanukah is clear. There is no difference between oil and vinegar, between one flask and eight, and between massive, fortified armies and a courageous few who were poorly trained for war. Everything is contingent on the *Ribono Shel Olam*, and everything He does is a *nes*.

In describing Klal Yisrael's war against Amalek, the *pasuk* says: "And when Moshe raised his hands toward Heaven, Yisrael advanced, and when he relaxed his hands, Amalek advanced."[46] The Mishnah asks: "Do the hands of Moshe wage war?" Certainly not![47]

The *pasuk* is teaching us that when the gaze of Klal Yisrael was focused high above and they humbled their hearts to their Father in Heaven, they were empowered; when it wasn't, they fell.

So have wars been fought throughout the history of Klal Yisrael, with the hand of Hashem leading the charge and with Hashem's miracles and wonders the implements of war. We have seen this phenomenon throughout *Tanach*, we have seen it in recent times in Eretz Yisrael, and we hope and we pray that the *Ribono Shel Olam* continues to protect His

---

45 Rabbi Chaim Shmuelevitz, *Sichos Mussar* 16.

46 *Shemos* 17:10.

47 *Rosh Hashanah* 29a.

people from all who wish their destruction with the same miracles and wonders that defeated the Greeks of long ago.

Some forty-two years ago, on Motzaei Shabbos Chanukah, I was *zocheh* to hear a young and promising *ben Torah* at Yeshivas Shor Yoshuv. Shmuel Davis, *z"l*, sing a *niggun* whose lyrics he wrote about the ongoing miracles in the *olam ha-teva* that we so often take for granted. The chorus was as follows:

A small wrinkled seed
Tiny and brown
Carefully sewn into place.
Give it a year, under the ground
And then it turns into a nes.

Unfortunately, a tragic automobile accident took that young man's life, but his message lives on and is celebrated yearly as we thank Hashem for the dual miracles of Chanukah.

In the liturgy of the kindling of the Chanukah lights, we sing: "*Uminosar kankanim na'aseh nes lashoshanim* — And from the one remnant of the flasks, a miracle was wrought for the roses (the *Chashmona'im*)."

When the Jewish people make themselves like *nosar*, a remnant, and they humble themselves to their Father in Heaven, or when they recognize in every aspect of their existence the continuous and miraculous infusion of the Hand of Hashem, then they are deserving of miracles of all types no less wondrous than the miracle of the efflorescence of the most beautiful rose.

CHAPTER 3

FORGETFULNESS: THE END OF THE BEGINNING

THE GIFT OF PILPULAH SHEL TORAH

Two elderly couples were enjoying friendly conversation over dinner one night when Charlie said to Fred, "By the way, Fred, I've been meaning to ask you — how was the memory clinic you visited last month?"

"Outstanding," Fred replied. "They taught us all of the latest psychological techniques: visualization, association, etc. It made a huge difference for me!"

"That's great, Fred!" Charlie said. "By the way, what was the name of the clinic?"

Fred went blank. He thought and he thought, but couldn't remember. After the passage of a few uncomfortable minutes, a smile broke across Fred's face and he asked, "Charlie, what do you call that long thing with pointy things sticking out, and with a red thing on top?"

"You mean a rose?" Charlie guessed.

"Yes! Yes!" Fred answered excitedly. "That's it! That's it! A rose!" Fred then turned to his wife and asked:

"Hey, Rose, what was the name of that clinic?"

UNFORTUNATELY, forgetfulness affects the senior population and can be terribly debilitating, drastically altering one's lifestyle. Thus, it is appropriate that we thank Hashem for maintaining our mental health.

There are times, however, when forgetting is actually a blessing in disguise. Would it not be for the "gift" of forgetfulness, we might always remember that awful, nauseous feeling we felt when we were sick (or post-Purim!) or the emotional pain we suffered at various losses and disappointments during the course of our lives. Nonetheless, everyone would agree that forgetting valuable information is to one's detriment (e.g., one's Social Security number, or the winning number on the lottery ticket). Certainly, the forgetting of Torah and the interruption of its clear transmission to future generations is a reason for concern.

This was the precise intent of the Greeks. "*L'hashkicham Torasecha* — To make them forget Your Torah" was their creed. The Yevanim darkened the eyes of Klal Yisrael with their decrees. The Hebrew word for darkness, *chasheichah*, is conspicuously related to the word *shich'chah*, forgetfulness, in that they have identical letters. In their brazen attempt to suggest an intellectual substitution for Torah, the Greeks were all-too successful. Many Jews bowed to Hellenistic influences and succumbed to their philosophies. In the wake of this academic attack on Klal Yisrael and Torah, the concentration essential for the proper transmission of the Torah was lost, and halachic disputes ensued. Indeed, the first recorded dispute of Tanna'im, that of Rabbi Yosi ben Yoezer and Rabbi Yosi ben Yochanan regarding the permissibility of doing *semichah* on Yom Tov, occurred during that period of history. This could have been the beginning of the end as the confusion that would ensue in its wake could have marked the ruination of the delicate process of proper retention and transmission of our holy Torah. But Hashem had other plans.[48]

---

48 Rabbi Yitzchak Hutner, *Pachad Yitzchak*, *Chanukah* 3.

Chazal tell us that sometimes what appears to be the *bitulah shel Torah*, the abrogation of Torah, proves to be its very *kiyum*, source of perpetuation.[49] Not only does the *refuah*, remedy, precede the *makah*, wound,[50] but sometimes the *refuah* is an actual outgrowth of the *makah*.[51] Unquestionably, the Greeks not only penetrated the physical *Heichal*, the Sanctuary of the Beis HaMikdash, but the human *heichal*, i.e., the Jewish mind as well. The numerical value of the word *heichal* is sixty-five, one less than *Yavan* (Greece), which is sixty-six.[52] Indeed, the Greeks were waging a fierce battle against that *heichal* and were winning the fight. *Shich'chas haTorah* was setting in, and the previously smooth transmission of the Torah was becoming dangerously clouded by *machlokes*.

However, what evolved from that precarious situation would prove to be the very tool that would deliver Torah to all future generations. That forgetfulness served as the catalyst to recapture the clarity of *Torah Sheba'al Peh*, the Oral Law, through a built-in methodology of analysis called *pilpulah shel Torah*, the debate of Torah that had became more prominent. By using the various principles with which the Torah is expounded — deliberation and discourse, vibrancy and excitement of the *milchamtah shel Torah*, intellectual battle of *chavrusos*, *shakla v'tarya*, and the give and take of the discussion characteristic of a *blatt Gemara* — the forgotten was restored and countless *chiddushei Torah*, novel Torah thoughts, were introduced in the process.

This newfound vibrancy in *limud haTorah* was not simply the redemption of Torah from the claws of *shich'chah*, but it became the light in the darkness and the foundation of the bridge that needed to be built to cross the threshold from those days (*ba-yamim ha-hem*) until the end of time (*ba-zman ha-zeh*).

Unfortunately, the victory over the Greeks was not complete. Their influence still reverberates today. The liberal influences of the universities and their effect on the moral decline in society has brought more darkness

49 *Menachos* 99b.

50 *Megillah* 13a.

51 *Mechilta, Beshalach* 15:25.

52 *Ne'os Hadesheh, Chanukah*.

to an already dark *galus*. The entertainment industry and the wide world of sports continue to thrive and thereby threaten to occupy our every free moment. Never has the Western world been so glittering and attractive. Survival requires a tremendous light that can persevere even in the thickness of this pitch blackness. It demands something so magnetic and enthralling that it would ward off the allurement of the deceptive *noy*, the attractiveness of Yavan (Yavan is *noy* spelled backwards, indicative of its obliquity).[53] The redeeming light represented by the Chanukah menorah is that of the *pilpulah shel Torah*, the *Torah Sheba'al Peh* on fire. It is the light of the *pasuk*: "*Ki ner mitzvah v'Torah ohr* — For a mitzvah is like a candle and Torah is light."[54]

Indeed, the Gemara in *Shabbos* asks, "*Mai Chanukah* — What is the Yom Tov of Chanukah all about? It responds with: "*D'tanu rabbanan* — The *rabbanan* taught in a *beraisah*," a hint to *Torah Sheba'al Peh* and the ensuing *pilpulah shel Torah*.[55] It is the light of the *pilpulah shel Torah* represented by the menorah lit outside, beneath ten *tefachim*, in the face of the forces of evil where the Shechinah does not descend,[56] in full view of the *galus*, which defies the odds and illuminates in spite of it all.[57] The light of the menorah emanates from the Beis HaMikdash as a last remnant of that holy place that overflowed with *kedushah* in a world saturated with *tumah*.[58] That light heralds the song that will bring to fruition the unfinished symphony at the ultimate *Chanukas Habayis Hashlishi*, the dedication of the third and final Beis HaMikdash. Then we will experience the fulfillment of the words of the *paytan*: *Az egmor b'shir mizmor chanukas hamizbe'ach* — Then I will conclude with a song, at the rededication of the altar."

At that moment, the symphony will be complete, and the whole world will sing in perfect harmony.

53 Ibid.

54 *Mishlei* 6:23.

55 *Shabbos* 21b.

56 *Sukkah* 5a.

57 *Ne'os Hadesheh* loc. cit.

58 Ramban to the beginning of *Parshas Beha'aloscha*.

CHAPTER 4

INSTANT KEDUSHAH

YES! THERE CAN BE PURITY IN THE FACE OF CATEGORICAL CONTAMINATION.

A man ran to the 24-hour convenience store at two in the morning, only to find the owner closing up for the night.

"What are you doing?" the man protested. "You can't be closing! Your sign says, 'Open 24 Hours!'"

"Yeah," the owner replied. "But not in a row!"

WE live in a world where everything is at our fingertips twenty-four hours a day, seven days a week, without interruption. One can shop to his heart's delight from the convenience of his home at any time of the day or night as long as he's online and has that indispensable piece of plastic — a credit card. Cars can be started and warmed up from the comfort of one's home; trunks pop open and car doors are unlocked with the push of a button on a key chain. The GPS or built-in navigation system precludes any need for asking directions (another lost *chesed* opportunity) as we cruise-control our way through the E-ZPass express toll at sixty miles an hour. The infamous TV remote control allows one to turn the TV on and off, change the channel, the station, the color, the contrast, the tone, the sound, and the decibel all from the comfort of one's bed. (As the story goes, a teenager asks his father: "Dad, is it true that when you were young you actually had to get up to change the channel?")

From the fax machine to the microwave, from the "clap your hands" light to the Shabbos lamp, comfort and convenience has become an expected way of life and, in the process, a mindset as well. We expect and demand everything to be instantaneous, and we quickly lose patience when it is not.

Unfortunately, this attitude affects our spirituality as well. We want instant *kedushah*, holiness. The popularization of such a distortion with books like *Kabbalah for the Layman* or through the promotion of Jewish mysticism to fill fleeting impulses for spirituality only exacerbates this twisted notion. Holiness is a gift from Hashem that only comes through tremendous effort on our parts. In the words of the *Mesilas Yesharim*: "The acquisition of holiness begins with effort and ends with a bequest from Heaven."[59]

Holiness is not something one simply studies. It is not purely academic. It is a lifetime occupation of serving Hashem, of scrupulous observance, of character improvement, of willpower, of withstanding temptation, and of the mastery of *nigleh*, the revealed Torah. Following that, it may be gifted to him with a gracious endowment of *siyata d'Shmaya*, as the Gemara in *Yoma* says: "A person who sanctifies himself a little bit, [Heaven] sanctifies him a lot."[60]

It seems almost ludicrous to speak about holiness in a world so saturated with all that is impure. In an atmosphere devoid of all restrictions and inundated with such open-mindedness that one has to wonder if the world's brains have fallen out, it is difficult to imagine any semblance of *kedushah* whatsoever. Yet, *Yisrael kedoshim hem*, the Jewish people are holy, and no matter the generation, no matter the climate

---

59 Rabbi Moshe Chaim Luzzato, *Mesilas Yesharim* 26.

60 *Yoma* 39a.

of the environment, they can nonetheless strive for and achieve their goal. Even in this decadent darkness, by toiling in Hashem's Torah and diligently keeping the mitzvos, a Jew can radiate light. And no matter where he finds himself, the Torah can serve as a beacon of light in the darkest of times for that light is powered by a higher Authority.

Chanukah, the last of the Yamim Tovim instituted until Mashiach comes, infused in Klal Yisrael the formula to bridge the gap until that auspicious moment.[61] Through the victory of a few courageous *Yidden* over the arrogance of the audacious Hellenists who dared to penetrate the Holy of Holies, we "absorbed" their brazenness and channeled it into an *azus d'kedushah*, a spiritual confidence that allows us to survive even in the face of wantonness and spiritual abandon.[62] The very fact that we light the Chanukah candles specifically outdoors, directly in the face of the darkness within ten *tefachim* of the ground, a place devoid of the Shechinah, and on the left side, which is traditionally associated with *kochos hatumah*, impure forces, is indication enough of this symbolism.[63] Armed with the ammunition of a rejuvenated *Torah Sheba'al Peh*, we carry the *azus d'kedushah* with great pride. We are also confident that we will persevere in this dark *galus*; that *kedushah* born out of sweat and travail will triumph and light the way until the time when the Shechinah will return to its abode with the arrival of Mashiach, speedily in our days.

---

61 *Pachad Yitzchak, Chanukah* 3.

62 *Ne'os Hadesheh* 1:160.

63 Ibid. 2:222.

Chapter 5

Where There's a Will, There's a Relationship

Yesh lanu chelek b'Elokei Yisrael.

A ninety-year-old man had serious hearing problems for a number of years. Finally, he went to the doctor and the doctor had him fitted for a set of the newest, most advanced miniscule hearing aids, implanted in the ear in such a way that they were barely noticeable. Amazingly, these devices allowed the gentleman to hear perfectly!

A month later, the senior citizen went back to the doctor. The doctor examined him and was extremely pleased. "Your hearing is perfect," he said. "Your family must be really pleased you can hear again."

The old man responded, "Oh, I haven't told my family yet. I just sit around and listen to their conversations. I've changed my will six times since then!"

ALTHOUGH the saying "Where there's a will, there are relatives" is humorous at best, it borders on an insight that is not only truthful but underscores the foundation of the Jewish soul. "Where there is a will, there is a ***relationship***," developed and nurtured, that can mark the difference between the mundane and the eternal. The letters of the Hebrew word *ratzon*, willpower, also spell the word *tzinor*, meaning pipeline or aqueduct. A sincere yearning (*ratzon*) of a spiritual nature creates a *tzinor* that allows the *chelek Elokah mi-ma'al* within to connect to the Source of it all above. This link permits one to transcend all of the limitations of a confined existence in this world and connect to *kochos* that defy limitations and exceed all boundaries. No longer is the "sky the limit," nor is one governed by *teva*, the natural world alone. The *ba'al ratzon* is transformed from one who relies on statistics to one who is steeped in the spirited conviction of the *pasuk*: "*Hayipalei m'Hashem davar*? — Is there anything too wondrous for Hashem to perform?"[64] He is no longer restricted to the dictum of *ein chadash tachas hashemesh* — there is nothing new under the sun,[65] but is part of a world that is *lema'alah min hashemesh* — above the sun, beyond the *olam ha-teva* where so much is new, for it is constantly renewed. He ceases to be a simple *yelud ishah*, a mere mortal (lit. "born of woman"), but a partner to the Eternal One, *Melech Malchei HaMelachim, HaKadosh Baruch Hu*.

The Mishnah in *Avos* instructs: "*Asei retzono k'retzonecha kedei sheya'aseh reztonchah k'retzono* — Treat His will as if it were your own will so that He will treat your will as if it were His will."[66] Clearly, uniting one's will with the *ratzon Hashem* creates an inseparable bond from which much benefit is reaped. It all begins with *ratzon*.

This *chelek* concept (that a Jew has a special connection to Hashem) was antithetical to all in which the Yevanim believed. To them, the *olam ha-teva* was where it was happening and man's intellect reigned supreme.

---

64 *Bereishis* 18:14.

65 *Koheles* 1:9.

66 *Avos* 2:4.

To think that man could supersede this world and latch on to a higher existence was anathema to their "celebration of mankind" doctrine.

So they decreed: "*Kisvu lachem al keren ha-shor she'ein lachem chelek b'Elokei Yisrael* — Write (these words) on the horn of an ox (and parade it through the marketplace) and proclaim that you have no *chelek* [i.e., no partnership] with the G-d of Israel."[67] Note their choice of words — no *chelek*. Enough of this fantasy about partnering with Hashem and connecting the *chelek Elokah* within to Hashem above, forget about transcending the limitations of the *olam ha-teva*, stop campaigning about a spiritual entity within that through the auspices of sincere *ratzon* creates a *tzinor* which impacts a *siyata d'Shmaya* beyond the comprehension of the human intellect.

They endeavored *l'ha'aviram mei-chukei retzonecha* — to make the Jews ignore a rule of thumb, a basic tenet of our belief, which is "*retzonecha* — Your will." They insisted that we relinquish our belief that it is all about Hashem's will and our will forging together as one; that it's all about creating that *tzinor*, for they knew that when that happens the odds no longer matter. We can be greatly outnumbered and yet nonetheless stand up proud and declare: *Yesh lanu chelek b'Elokei Yisrael.* We can pronounce to the world our unequivocal belief in the conviction of Dovid HaMelech: "*Eileh va-rechev v'eileh ba-susim va-anachnu b'shem Hashem Elokeinu nazkir. Hemah karu v'nafalu va-anachnu kamnu va-nis'odad* — Some with chariots, and some with horses, but we, in the name of Hashem our G-d, we call out. They slumped and fell but we arose and were invigorated."[68]

---

67 *Bereishis Rabbah* 2:5.

68 *Tehillim* 20:8–9.

Chapter 6

The Influence of Outside Elements

Overpowering the Lure of the Marketplaces of the World

Joe Smith started the day early, having set his alarm clock (MADE IN JAPAN) for 6 a.m. While his coffee pot (MADE IN CHINA) was percolating, he shaved with his electric razor (MADE IN HONG KONG). He put on a dress shirt (MADE IN SRI LANKA), designer jeans (MADE IN SINGAPORE), and tennis shoes (MADE IN KOREA).

After cooking his breakfast in his new electric skillet (MADE IN INDIA), he sat down with his calculator (MADE IN MEXICO) to see how much he could spend today. After setting his watch (MADE IN TAIWAN) to the radio (MADE IN LAOS), he got in his car (MADE IN GERMANY) and continued his search for a good-paying AMERICAN job.

At the end of yet another discouraging and fruitless day, Joe decided to relax for a while. He put on his sandals (MADE IN BRAZIL), poured himself a glass of wine (MADE

> *IN FRANCE), turned on his TV (MADE IN INDONESIA), and then wondered why he can't find a good paying job in... AMERICA.*

SOME might refer to this imbalance as a sell-out to the low-priced labor of foreign markets at the expense of the American citizenry motivated by greed and self-indulgence. Others may argue: Why manufacture an item in America if it costs half the price elsewhere? It's simply good business sense. Whatever the case, there's no doubt that as a result the unemployment figures are high and jobs are scarce. It is hard to compete with the magnetic lure of the cost-effective workforces of the marketplaces of the world.

The challenges of the marketplace don't end there. From the days of the Yevanim, *ad hayom ha-zeh*, until this very day, our spirituality is threatened by the unremitting influences from the *shuk*, marketplace. The bombardment is both invited and uninvited. With the advent of Internet connections, the *shuk* is at one's fingertips to be summoned at one's whim. Through it one can find every conceivable decadence and fantasy. All the destructive forces that are inextricably part of today's world scene are his to enjoy (more properly, to destroy his *ruchnius*) right there in the comfort of his home without even lifting his physical being to enter their *shuk*. Our homes have been penetrated, our minds have been inundated, our hearts have been infiltrated. We are victim to a *regilus min hashuk* — relentless influences from the marketplace that is unparalleled in the history of mankind.

In the *Al Hanisim* prayer, it mentions how in the aftermath of the victory of the Jews over the Yevanim, we cleaned up the *Heichal* and lit the *neros* of the menorah "*b'chatzros kadshecha* — in the courtyard of Your holy sanctuary." The prayer continues: "*V'kavu shemonas yemei Chanukah eilu l'hodos u'l'hallel l'Shimcha ha-gadol* — And they established these eight days of Chanukah to praise and sing *Hallel* to Your holy name." The Chasam Sofer connects these adjacent phrases in an attempt to answer the well-known question of the Beis Yosef, who asked why we celebrate Chanukah for eight days when, in fact, they possessed enough oil for one night [and thereby the miracle really only lasted seven days].

The Chasam Sofer begins his answer by asking another obvious question on the *nusach* of the *Al Hanisim* cited above that states that they lit the menorah **in the courtyard** of the Beis HaMikdash. He asks: since when is the menorah lit in the courtyard and not in the *Heichal* itself?

It must be that they found lighting the menorah in the *Heichal* prohibitive because of the destruction there and therefore moved it outside to be lit in the courtyard. But when lighting outside in a courtyard, one would need more oil than normal because of the atmospheric elements that the lights are subject to in an unprotected environment. Indeed, that one flask of oil would have sufficed had they lit inside, but being that they were forced to light outside in the courtyard, those lights were subject to the outside atmospheric components, thereby necessitating more oil than what was found in that one flask.

It follows that there was, in fact, a miracle the first night of Chanukah as well. The words of the *Al Hanisim* are precise and address the very dilemma of the Beis Yosef: Because on that particular night they were forced to light the menorah outdoors in the courtyard of the Beis HaMikdash with a limited supply of oil (i.e., not enough to burn an entire night under the influence of the outdoor elements), and nonetheless it burned through the entire night, they therefore established eight days of Chanukah and not merely seven days, for a miracle occurred the first night as well.

Based on the above, the *nes* of the menorah represents a victory over the outside elements and interferences that plague us until this very day. It fits well that the *shiur* of the burning of the Chanukah *licht* is "*ad shetichleh regel min hashuk* — until the marketplace has emptied of its constituency." It was those very elements from the *shuk* that the Yevanim were pushing down the throats of a vulnerable Klal Yisrael as the way to live life to its fullest. Many a Jew succumbed to their inundation. After all, it was very attractive and alluring; it was inclusive and inviting. The very name of this nation that tried to convert the Jewish people to their way of thinking was Yavan, whose Hebrew letters — *yud, vav, nun* — spell *noy* (*nun, vav, yud*), which means attractive and enthralling, fascinating and appealing. The draw was strong, but a few brave Jews stood up for truth and didn't allow the *regel min hashuk* in. The Chanukah *licht* burned through the night as a testimony to the *siyata d'Shmaya* accessible to one who wishes to swim against the tide and aspire for purity in the face of darkness, no matter how mesmerizing and "bright" it may appear to be.

We may benefit from all types of products produced in marketplaces throughout the world, but we dare not forget that *we* are not made in China, Germany, Japan, or America, but in *Shamayim*, where our soul is fashioned in the very image of Hashem, and whose purpose it is to illuminate the *shuk* — the outside world that threatens to consume us — with the light of the Torah, so brilliant that all else pales in comparison.

Chapter 7

More Than My Portion

L'hodos u'l'hallel l'Shimcha ha-gadol

Every morning, a devoted religious woman would open her front door and scream, "Praise the Lord!"

This annoyed her atheist neighbor, who would counter, "There is no Lord!"

One day, the atheist neighbor overheard his religious neighbor praying for food. Thinking it would be funny, he bought her all sorts of groceries and then left them on her porch.

Of course, the next morning the religious lady opened her door and screamed, "Praise the Lord!" Noticing the groceries, she added, "Who gave me this bounty of food."

The laughing neighbor could barely get the words out and screamed, "It wasn't the Lord — it was me!"

Without missing a beat, she screamed, "Praise the Lord for giving me this bounty of food — and for making the atheist next door pay for it."

THE definition of *hoda'ah*, thanksgiving, is well expressed by Rashi in *Chumash* in the name of the *Midrash Rabbah*. In explanation of Leah's decision to name her fourth son Yehudah, Leah said, "*Ha-pa'am odeh es Hashem* — This time I will give thanks to Hashem,"[69] and accordingly named him Yehudah ("*Al ken karah shemo Yehudah* — She therefore called his name Yehudah.") Rashi explains: *Shenatalti yoseir mechelki me'atah yesh li l'hodos* — For I have received more than my portion and therefore I am required to give thanks." With the birth of a fourth son, one more than Leah envisioned as a four-way partner in the twelve *shivtei Kah* (Yaakov Avinu had four wives), she felt compelled to thank Hashem.

At first glance, it seems somewhat peculiar that Leah would only thank Hashem after receiving **more** than her portion. Wouldn't the birth of even one precious child be ample reason to be filled with thanksgiving? Aren't we to be appreciative for all that we receive from Hashem on an ongoing basis? Does the *Eibishter* owe us anything? Isn't this world from its inception *yesh me'ayin*, substance from nothingness, and an unending *chesed* of Hashem? And, finally, shouldn't we expect more from someone on the caliber of one of the *imahos*, matriarchs?

Perhaps we can suggest the following: It goes without saying that our matriarch Leah had the sensitivity and foresight to thank the *Ribono Shel Olam* for everything in life. Undoubtedly, she was filled with thanks for every one of her children. Nonetheless, she waited to utilize the expression of *hoda'ah* for this auspicious occasion (i.e., the birth of her fourth son Yehudah, when it was clear that she had indeed received more than her portion of the *shivtei Kah*) in order to teach us the following pedagogical lesson for life: the definition of *hoda'ah* is to sincerely feel that **everything** we receive from Hashem — from the smallest to the most impressive — is **more than our portion**. The quintessential thanksgiving is one that is replete with the humility that declares: "Hashem, You owe me nothing! All that You give me is more than my portion. I humble myself before You, for every breath that I take is from Your goodness!" Indeed, the name Yehudah is an acronym

69 *Bereishis* 29:35.

for the *shem Hashem*, *yud-hei-vav*, *hei*, and a *daled*, which represents the *dal* — poor man, as if to proclaim: I stand before You, Hashem, like a *dal* who is totally humbled before his benefactor.

A similar idea might explain the juxtaposition of two expressions in the first *berachah* of the *Shemoneh Esrei*. We praise Hashem with the expression "*Gomel chasadim tovim* — Who bestows beneficial kindnesses," followed by the expression "*v'Konei hakol* — and Who creates everything." The *semichus*, association, is obvious. Even though Hashem created and owns everything, and owes us nothing whatsoever, He nonetheless bestows all of this kindness every moment of our existence. For this reason, we are enormously humbled before Him and proclaim our gratitude for having received more than our portion, more than once, more than we can count.

Chanukah was established for future generations *l'hodos u'l'hallel* — to express thanks and praise. Having learned the definition of *hoda'ah* as a keen understanding that everything we receive is more than our portion, we are ready to say *Hallel*.

Hallel declares that we will never forget that we are in the realm of a *dal* before Hashem. Even when Hashem lifts us up and grants us great distinction as the *mamleches Kohanim v'goy kadosh* — nation of priests and a holy nation; even when we represent the aristocracy and nobility of the world; even as the prime example of the majesty of man — as kings and queens, princes and princesses; even when we are *malchus mamash* like Dovid HaMelech before us, we humble ourselves before Him with the greatest of humility. Even though Hashem "*mekimi meafar dal me'ashpos yarim evyon* — raises the needy from the dust and from the trash heaps He lifts the destitute,"[70] we nonetheless will not allow his graciousness to remove us from the realization that we are but *dal* and *evyon*, humbled before our Master.

Sefer Tehillim, written by Dovid HaMelech, is a case in point. The entire *sefer* demonstrates that true majesty comes when one is humble before his Creator, like its author. The very name Dovid, spelled *daled*

---

70 *Tehillim* 113:7.

vav daled, indicates this. The first *daled* represents the humility of a *dal*. The *vav* is the *vav hachibur* (the function of the *vav* when it connects two things) that symbolizes the greatness of man when he connects his *chelek Elokah mi-ma'al* to the *Ribono Shel Olam* above. Even after he has risen to this level that is G-dly and majestic, he still remains a *dal*, as represented by the last *daled*.[71]

The *Avnei Nezer* explains that such is our *avodah* on the Yom Tov of Chanukah. He asks: Why did the *nes* of Chanukah occur with oil? Because the nature of oil is such that as it diminishes and dissipates it produces light. Our task in life is to produce a great symphony. On the one hand, we generate abundant light and achieve greatness. But as we do so, we also become more and more humbled before Hashem, the Source of all light and to Whom we offer continuous *hallel v'hoda'ah* for granting us much, much more than our portion.

---

71 *Ohr Gedalyahu, Chanukah*, pg. 76.

Chapter 8

The Innocence of Youth

Girsa D'yankusa — Learning with a Clean Slate

It was the final round of the $64,000 question and only three remaining contestants were left: an Englishman, a Texan, and an Arkansan.

The M.C. began: "The question is: finish the following song title and spell the answer. "Old Macdonald had a _____."

The Englishman goes first and responds, "estate," spelling it "e-s-t-a-t-e."

The M.C. says, "Sorry. Wrong answer, but right spelling."

Meanwhile, the Arkansan is going nuts with excitement to the point that he can hardly control himself.

The Texan goes next and answers, "ranch," spelling it "r-a-n-c-h."

Again, the M.C. says, "Sorry. Wrong answer, but right spelling."

By now, the Arkansan is jumping up and down, so excited he almost screams.

The M.C. turns to the Arkansan and says, "O.K., for $64,000 can you tell us what Old Macdonald had and spell your answer?

The Arkansan answers with confidence, "Farm, e-i-e-i-o!"

WE are all indelibly impressed by what we learn in our youth. Having absorbed the information at a time when our heads weren't so clouded and cluttered, when we had a clean slate, the information goes in quicker and stays with us longer. A familiar example of this phenomenon is manifest in the vast difference between children and their parents in their ability to learn Hebrew upon making *aliyah* to Eretz Yisrael. While the parents struggle with their new dialect for years (perhaps even decades), their small children master the foreign vernacular in a matter of months, together with the accent and even the rolling of the *resh*. *Chazal* called this phenomenon *girsah d'yankusah*, the natural learning (and internalization) of one's youth.

The Gemara in the beginning of the *sugya* that relates to Chanukah makes mention of this idea.[72] At the end of the discussion whether it is necessary to relight the Chanukah *licht* should they extinguish prior to their burning the requisite *shiur* of time,[73] the Gemara quotes the opinion of Rav. He says that although one may not use inferior wicks and oil for Shabbos *licht*, he may use them throughout Chanukah without concern for their substandard ability to light.

Rav Yirmiyah explains Rav's reasoning for this decision as follows: "He holds *kavsah ein zakuk lah* — if the Chanukah *licht* extinguish prematurely one is not obligated (*zakuk* meaning "attached") to relight them, and *asur l'hishtamesh l'orah* — that it is generally forbidden to benefit from their light." Therefore, one need not be concerned about the inferiority of the wicks or oils, for were the lights to extinguish early and he would not relight them, he still would fulfill the mitzvah. In addition, on Shabbos Chanukah, one may use those same wicks and

---

72 *Shabbos* 21b.

73 Assuming enough oil was used to potentially burn for half an hour.

oils without concern of *shema yateh*, that he might be tempted to adjust the lamp due to the poor quality of their light, for he is not permitted to use the *ner* of Chanukah for his mundane purposes.

The Gemara continues: The Rabbanan repeated Rav Yirmiyah's explanation of Rav's opinion before Abaya, but he would not accept it because he did not consider Rav Yirmiyah sufficiently worthy to rely on his words.[74] Sometime later, when Ravin came from Eretz Yisrael to Bavel, the very same explanation of Rav's opinion was said over before Abaya in the name of Rav Yochanan and this time he accepted it as the law.

Abaya then lamented: "Had I merited, I would have accepted this explanation previously when I heard it the first time in the name of Rav Yirmiyah!" To which the Gemara asks: "[What difference does it make?] In the end, he did accept it and incorporated it into his learning."

The Gemara responds: "*Nafka minah l'girsa d'yankusa*" — there is a difference, for had Abaya accepted this statement earlier in life, he would have learned it when he was younger with a cleaner slate, making its perpetuation possibly that much greater. And although it is not clear from the Gemara how much time had transpired between the first time Abaya heard this *p'shat* and the second time (was it years, months, or just days?), it seems that the loss of *girsa d'yankusa* is to be bemoaned, no matter the interval.

One might ask: Why is this dictum taught to us specifically in the *sugya* of Chanukah? What special connection does *girsa d'yankusa* have to Chanukah?

Chanukah receives its name *al shem* the *Chanukas Hamizbe'ach*, the rededication of the Temple. The obvious link to *chinuch* is manifest in the fact that they were unwilling to rely on leniencies. The principle of *tumah hutrah b'tzibur* — that if the majority of the congregation is *tamei* we may forgo on the laws of *tumah* — would have permitted them to use *tamei* oil. *Ein shiur l'ovei hapesilos* — there is no precise required thickness for the diameter of the wicks, and so making the wicks seven-eighths thinner would have allowed the one flask to be enough for eight days.

74 Rashi there.

Either would have eliminated the need for a miracle. However, when it comes to *chinuch*, to beginning anew, we are not satisfied with anything but the best. With the education of our children, we must lay the foundation in the most preferred fashion.

Just as youth is wonderfully refreshing, so is all renewal. The Yom Tov of Chanukah provides an opportunity for a metamorphosis that refreshes and rejuvenates. The *or haganuz* of *Ma'aseh Bereishis* hidden away for *tzaddikim* finds its way to the Chanukah menorah and illuminates and shines. The thirty-six candles that we light over the course of the eight days of Chanukah are symbolic of the thirty-six *mesechtos* in *Shas* that have Gemara,[75] as well as the thirty-six hidden *tzaddikim* of every generation. The Beis HaMikdash and all its magnificence come alive, as the only remnant of the *avodah* endures in the Chanukah *licht*.[76]

Like that young child beginning the *chinuch* process, we all become pure again. Inspired by the absolute belief that *kavsah* — even if the flame of *Yiddishkeit* has been somewhat extinguished and has lost its vitality — *ein zakuk lah*, we are not attached to that thought. We regain our resolve; we do not despair. We believe that the flame can be reignited — that once again we can be pure, and we can light up the world until the menorah will be lit once again in the Beis HaMikdash, *b'vias goel tzedek bimheirah*.

75 *Ohr Gedalyahu*, Chanukah, pg.77; *Shem Mishmuel*, Chanukah.

76 Ramban to the beginning of *Parshas Beha'aloscha*.

Chapter 9

It Only Gets Better

Mehadrin min Hamehadrin — The Hiddur Mitzvah of Limud HaTorah — Chazarah

A group of fifteen-year-old girlfriends decided to meet for dinner. They discussed where to eat and finally agreed on a fast-food joint next to the Sea Side Restaurant because they only had fifteen dollars between them.

Ten years later, the same girlfriends, now twenty-five years old, discussed where to meet for dinner. Finally, they agreed to meet at the Sea Side Restaurant because it had free snacks, there was no cover charge, the beer was cheap, and the band was good.

Ten years later, the same girlfriends, now thirty-five years old, discussed where to meet for dinner. Finally, they agreed to meet at the Sea Side Restaurant because the combos were good, it was near the gym, and if they went late enough there wouldn't be many whiny small children.

Ten years later, the same girlfriends, now forty-five years old, discussed where to meet for dinner. Finally, they agreed to meet at the Sea Side Restaurant because the martinis were large and it had a great salad bar.

Ten years later, the same girlfriends, now fifty-five years old, discussed where to meet for dinner. Finally they agreed to meet at the Sea Side Restaurant because the prices were reasonable, the wine list was good, and fish was good for their cholesterol.

Ten years later, the same girlfriends, now sixty-five years old, discussed where to meet for dinner. Finally, they agreed to meet at the Sea Side Restaurant because they had an Early Bird Special, the lighting was good, and they had a special senior discount.

Ten years later, the same girlfriends, now seventy-five years old, discussed where to meet for dinner. Finally, they agreed to meet at the Sea Side Restaurant because the food wasn't too spicy and it was wheelchair accessible.

Ten years later, the same girlfriends, now eighty-five years old, discussed where to meet for dinner. Finally, they agreed to meet at the Sea Side Restaurant because they had never been there before.

MY *rebbi*, Harav Shlomo Freifeld, *zt"l*, would often repeat the story about Harav Tzvi Pesach Frank, *zt"l*, the great Chief Rabbi of Yerushalayim fifty years ago and his loyal *chavrusa* who had studied *Meseches Chulin* sixty times together. Upon completing *Chulin* for the sixtieth time, the *chavrusa* asked Rav Tzvi Pesach what they would be learning next. The Rav answered in a very matter-of-fact manner, "*Chulin.*" The *chavrusa* respectfully told Rav Tzvi Pesach that he needs a change in the subject matter and can't learn *Chulin* again right now. Rav Tzvi Pesach responded: "I understand. I'll find another *chavrusa*," which he found immediately.

Rav Tzvi Pesach began the *mesechta* again with his new *chavrusa*, articulating and translating each and every word as if he had never learned *Chulin* before. "*Hakol shochtin*, everyone is permitted to slaughter; *chutz*, except; *m'cheresh shoteh v'katan*, for a deaf mute, an insane person, and a minor..." And so it continued.

To great *talmidei chachamim*, there was no such thing as having been there already or of having learned that previously. Torah to them was always new, *k'yom shenitnah b'Har Sinai* — like the day it was given at Har Sinai, for it was the vernacular of Hashem Who is *mechadesh b'tuvo b'chol yom tamid ma'aseh bereishis*.

It is well known that of all of the mitzvos, the study of Torah reigns supreme. Our learning is something we hold on to for dear life, for it is our life. Yet, if our learning is of the "it goes in one ear and then out the other" variety, it loses its vitality both from the perspective of its effect and of its reward. We desperately need to learn the importance of *chazarah*, review, as the mainstay of the fulfillment of learning Torah. This is where we often encounter the "same-thing syndrome."

The "same-thing syndrome" is an ailment that affects many who, to their credit, may study Torah regularly but suffer from the attitude of "I've learned that before; I can't learn it again. I must learn something new, something I've never learned before. There's so much to learn, I don't have time to review."

Chazal tell us that just the opposite is true. They explain, regarding what appears to be a redundancy in the *pasuk* that says "*Im shamoa tishma* — If you will surely listen,"[77] that if you learn the old information well (through constant review), then the new information will be understood with much more ease. The acquisition of the old studies, through the toil of constant *chazarah*, will not only facilitate the acquisition of the new studies with greater ease but will bring a surge of *siyata d'Shmaya* that will make the unfathomable yours and the unreachable within your grasp.

The importance of review underscores the ultimate goal of Torah study, which is *kinyan haTorah*, the acquisition of Torah. Our task is not merely to study Torah but to acquire it — to make it ours. In discussing

---

77 *Devarim* 11:13.

the issue of whether a *talmid chacham* has the right to be *mochel* on his *kavod* — to relinquish on the honor he is due, the Gemara attempts to bring a proof for such a right from the *Ribono Shel Olam* Himself Who so humbly acted as a personal guide for Bnei Yisrael in the desert.[78] The Gemara immediately objects that we can't learn from Hashem's willingness to yield His honor, because the world is His and the Torah is His, and therefore their honor is within His jurisdiction to concede, as opposed to the *talmid chacham* who has no such dominion. Rava responds that indeed the honor of the Torah is the *talmid chacham*'s to renounce, for the Torah is his once he learns it repeatedly and has acquired it. At first, it is the Torah of Hashem, but after a concerted effort on the part of the Torah scholar to acquire his learning, it becomes his. The true *talmid chacham* takes his Torah with him wherever he goes, for it is his, embedded in his mind and implanted in his heart.

Chazal teach us in *Berachos*: "*Igra d'pirka rihata* — The primary reward for the studying of Torah at the *shiur* is for the energy expended in running to the *shiur*."[79] The question is conspicuous: Shouldn't the primary reward for the study of Torah be for the study of Torah itself? Rashi once again comes to the rescue. He explains why the primary reward is the reward for running to the *drashah* and not the *s'char limud*. The reason is: "*Sheharei ruban einam mevinim* — that most of the people attending the *shiur* do not understand the *drashah* well enough to remember its text [to be able to] repeat it properly in the name of their *rebbi* at a later date, for which they would have received the more cherished reward for the learning of Torah."

Rashi's words are monumental yet frightening. To think that the most coveted reward we seek is so easily lost without proper retention is terrifying! This places a great responsibility upon us to acquire our learning so that it is inscribed in our memory bank, secured for eternity.

The Gemara in *Berachos* discusses the *chassidim harishonim*, the early righteous ones, who would spend nine hours a day involved in

---

78 *Kiddushin* 32a.

79 *Berachos* 6b.

prayer.[80] The Gemara questions the limitations that this practice would place on their time to learn Torah, but the Gemara never asks the more obvious question: when did they have time to learn? Rather it asks: *Torasan he'ach mishtameres*, how did they retain their Torah? How was their Torah guarded in their memories when they had so little time to review what they had learned?[81] The Gemara's focus is on the review, their *kinyan haTorah*, for that is primary.

Purim and Chanukah are the exclusive *yamim tovim derabanan* — rabbinically instituted holidays, which help pave the way for our survival in *galus*, bridging the gap until the coming of Mashiach. Each of these Yamim Tovim focuses on Torah in its own way. The amazing revelation on Purim brought about an acceptance of the Torah from Klal Yisrael's love for Hashem and His miracles, an acceptance that surpassed the one at Har Sinai, as Chazal say: *hadar kibluhah* — the Jews voluntarily reaccepted the Torah after the events of *Megillas Esther.*[82] Through the events of Chanukah, the *Torah Sheba'al Peh* became ever more prominent as the panacea to protect against the forgetting of Torah until this very day.

The unusual ecumenical acceptance of the *mehadrin min hamehadrin*, the most glorified manner of performing the mitzvah of lighting Chanukah candles, may very well be linked to the idea that Klal Yisrael didn't really require a miracle when they wanted to reinaugurate the menorah. After all, the law is *tumah hutrah b'tzibur* — if the majority of the people are contaminated, the laws of spiritual impurity are relaxed. In addition, there is no absolute requirement for the thickness of the wicks. The victorious Jews could have used the impure oil or have made the wicks seven-eighths thinner so as to burn less oil until new oil could be procured. One reason that they did not was that to use such oil would have detracted from the beauty of the mitzvah. Because the miracle of Chanukah may have been motivated by their insistence to be *mehader b'mitzvos*, to beautify the mitzvah, there evolved the universal

---

80 Ibid. 32b.

81 *Maharsha* to ibid.

82 *Shabbos* 88a.

commitment to perform this mitzvah in the most preferred and enhanced fashion, *mehadrin min hamehadrin*.

If Chanukah marks the beginning of the power of the light of the *Torah Sheba'al Peh* to illuminate the darkness of the impending *galus* through the *pilpulah shel Torah*, as well as a time when the enhancement of a mitzvah played a pivotal role in the events of the day, then it is a time when we must focus on how to be *mehader*, to enhance our study of Torah. What greater *hiddur* could there be in the learning of Torah than the constant review of Torah? Indeed, in Aramaic the word *mehader* means "to return" or "to review."

Perhaps this too is the meaning of Chazal regarding Klal Yisrael's reacceptance of the Torah after the story of Purim. *Hadar kibluhah* — the *kabbalas haTorah* of Purim was one of *hadar*, review. The clarity they enjoyed and their love for Hashem and His Torah that ensued from the miracle of Purim inspired them to accept upon themselves to learn Torah with an absolute commitment to make it theirs forever.

Through the *kinyan haTorah*, the acquisition of what we learn, we can take the Torah we have learned into the darkness of *galus* with a renewed confidence that it will protect us in this world and be our delight in the World to Come.

Chapter 10

The Positives and the Negatives of Brazenness

Ga'avah d'Kedushah as a Tool in Avodas Hashem

A well-known funnyman once said, "I don't get no respect. Even my dog doesn't respect me. He keeps barking at the front door, but not because he wants to go out.

"He wants me to leave."

"MAN'S best friend" might be less of a friend and more a competitor than we think. The Hebrew word for dog, *kelev*, says as much: *kelev lashon ki lev* — an expression of like a heart, but not a real heart. A dog has the audacity to imply some type of equivalence to man, his master, and this smells from brazenness. He will even walk before his "master." Nonetheless, he is not the most brazen among the beasts. That distinction Chazal tell us belongs to the *namer*, the leopard. This animal is so barefaced and bold that it attacks other beasts much more powerful than it. Unlike the other animals in the animal kingdom, it doesn't recognize its position.

The Torah alludes to the four empires that will rule over Klal Yisrael (the four *galios*) in a *pasuk* in *Bereishis*: "*Veha'aretz haisah sohu vavohu v'choshech al pinei tehom* — And the earth was empty and void and there was darkness on the face of the depths."[83] *Sohu* is the *malchus* of Bavel; *vohu*, the *malchus* of Paras (Persia); *choshech*, the *malchus* of Yavan (Greece); and *tehom*, the *malchus* of Edom (Rome).[84] Yavan is compared to darkness because they darkened the eyes of the Jews with their *gezeros*. Less known is the *pasuk* in *Daniel* that allegorically alludes to the four *malchios* as various beasts. Third among them is the *namer*, the animal equivalent of the Greeks, so compared because of their unprecedented brazenness.

Many a nation had tried to destroy us physically, but never had one been as audacious to profess a way of life superior to the Torah as the Yevanim did. They were so audacious as to penetrate the *Heichal* and defile it.[85] They were successful in influencing thousands of Jews, imposing their philosophy, their academics, and their approach to life as the way to go for all of mankind, from the most base to the most intelligent. Their worship of the *seichel enushi*, the intellect of man, spread like wildfire and became a comfortable alternative to all too many Hellenists who sold out to their inducement. To suggest that *chachmas Yevanis* was on par with Torah was a chutzpah beyond belief, yet until a few courageous Chasmona'im stepped up to the plate, subsuming the enemy's very weapon of brazenness in the form of *ga'avah d'Kedushah*, the battle was almost lost. *Baruch Hashem*, the Chashmona'im persevered and removed their influence from the *Heichal* of the Beis HaMikdash and the minds of a Klal Yisrael threatened with spiritual annihilation.

Yehudah ben Teimah said, "*Hevei az k'namer...la'asos ratzon Avichah shebaShamayim* — Be bold as a leopard...to carry out the will

83 *Bereishis* 1:2.

84 *Bereishis Rabbah* 2:4.

85 *Yavan* in *gematria* is sixty-six, while *heichal* is sixty-five.

of your Father in Heaven." In the very next Mishnah, he continues: "*Az panim l'gehinnom* — The brazen one goes to Gehinnom."[86] This appalling *middah* of *azus*, brazenness, obviously has its positive attributes when applied to the fulfillment of the will of Hashem. In fact, by virtue of the victory of the Chashmana'im over the Yevanim, they conquered the *middah ra'ah* of *azus* and converted it to a *ga'avah d'Kedushah* that would serve Klal Yisrael well for all future generations. We are proud Jews delighted with our portion in life to serve the *Ribono Shel Olam* and to adhere to His Torah. And although this pride often manifests itself in the realm of mere *chitzonius* (e.g., our outward appearance — beards and *payos*, *tzitzis* out, hats and jackets, *tznius* and modest attire, snoods and kerchiefs) nonetheless, *chitzonius* is *me'orer penimius* — the exterior is meant to inspire the interior with a compelling feeling in one's heart that the greatest privilege known to man is to humble oneself before Hashem.

With *ga'avah d'Kedushah* comes a *siyata d'Shmaya* that defies all mathematics and statistics. Neither the massive numbers of the Greek armies nor the overwhelming numbers of Jews who had caved in to the influences of the Yevanim mattered. What mattered was the degree of devotion to Hashem and dedication to His Torah. Then, all would fall into place. Indeed, the *mispar katan gematria* of Chashmona'im when spelled *chaser* without the *vav* (the *ches* is eight, the *shin* is three, the *mem* is four, the *nun* is five, the *aleph* is one, the *yud* is one, and the *mem* is four) is twenty-six, the equivalent of the *Shem HaVaYa*, the very name of Hashem. Yes, the Yevanim had penetrated the *Heichal* and the score was sixty-six to sixty-five in their favor, but when the Chashmona'im demonstrated their *ga'avah d'Kedushah*, the numbers no longer mattered, for they connected to Hashem (twenty-six) and were *zocheh* to *siyata d'Shmaya*.

Unfortunately, the victory over the Yevanim was never complete. It is only through the *ga'avah d'Kedushah* of the Chashmona'im throughout the generations that we have survived the darkness of the *galus*

86 *Avos* 5:23.

promulgated by the Greeks that continues to prevail upon us to this very day. The *mispar katan* of the Hebrew word *choshech*, darkness, is thirteen, as is the *gematria* of the word *echad*, one.[87] May we merit living to see the end of that influence and a time when the entire world will proclaim with the greatest of pride and joy the truth about the Oneness of Hashem,[88] His Torah, and His people, *b'vias go'el tzedek bimheirah b'yameinu*!

87 *Ches* is eight, *shin* is three, and *chaf* is two.

88 *Echad* — *aleph, ches, daled* — in the *mispar katan gematria* is also thirteen.

CHAPTER 11

SPEAK UP FOR TRUTH AND SAVE LIVES

A WAR OF TWISTED WORDS AND TRUTH

Yankel passes by a pet shop and noticed a parrot in the window selling for $1,500. Upon entering the store, he asks the proprietor why the parrot is so expensive.

"Are you kidding?" asks the storeowner. "That parrot speaks five languages!"

"Does it speak Yiddish?" asks Yankel, thinking how it would make a wonderful companion for his elderly mother who lived alone.

"Sure does!" said the owner.

Yankel decides to buy the parrot as a present for his mother, pays the $1,500, and arranges for the shop to have it delivered directly to her address.

The next day, Yankel calls his mother and asks: "Mom, how do you like the parrot I bought you?"

"Mmm, it was delicious," she answers.

"What do you mean delicious?" Yankel exclaims.

"I made soup out of it. It came out great!" says his mother.

"Ma," cries Yankel. "That parrot wasn't for eating. It was a special bird. It spoke five languages! It even spoke Yiddish!"

After a short pause, his mother replies, "Nu, so why didn't it say something?"

THE Gemara in *Makkos*, in discussing the advantage of two *talmidei chachamim* escorting an unwitting murderer to the *arei miklat*, cities of refuge, notes that they will be able to speak up in his defense if confronted by the *goel hadam*, the enraged relative (lit., the redeemer of the blood). In response to a question as to why it wouldn't be more beneficial for the murderer to speak on his own behalf, the Gemara says: "*Harbei shluchin osin* — Much more can be accomplished by agents."[89] That is to say, the murderer is better off through the defensive arguments of uninvolved parties, especially if they are respected Torah scholars. Needless to say, lives can be saved through a well-articulated defense of the innocent party. But it's not always so easy.

Just a few short years ago, a war raged in Gaza between Israel and Hamas that was being fought not only on the battlefield but on the television screen as well. Many intelligent people who went to the best universities, who grew up and live in democratic societies, and who once upon a time took pride in honest journalism that presented the truth, (even some progressive Jews) had become the bastion of bias and the criticism of Klal Yisrael. It was hard to believe that it was CBS, CNN, or the BBC reporting and not Al-Jazeera or Pravda. The one-sidedness and overt anti-Semitism was horrendous. The blatant lies and devastating shifts of information on the part of the media at large granted legitimacy to terrorists and cold-blooded murderers. The raining down of thousands of missiles aimed at innocent civilians (men, women, and children) was equated with a necessary defense by Israel, the victim. The aggressor

89 *Makkos* 10b.

became the victim and the victim the aggressor to the point of charges of war crimes and genocide. Israel was even criticized for possessing the Iron Dome anti-missile defense system, for is it fair that they have access to such apparatus when the terrorists do not?

The distortion is so blatant that it makes one shudder at the memory of the lies spread around the world, of the propaganda unleashed that led to a Holocaust and the destruction of six million. When the President of the United States of America suggests that two countries that openly espouse their support of terrorism and their goal to eradicate all Jews from the face of the earth act in the capacity as "honest brokers" of a ceasefire, you begin to believe that there is no one left to speak on our behalf.

We pray that Hashem sends the proper *sheluchim*, agents, who exhibit the courage to speak the truth and help maintain a semblance of balance in a world gone mad (may Hashem save us).

Sometimes, it just takes a few honest spokesmen to change the tide and alter destiny. A few people who say it as it is can change the course of history. Such is the power of truth. Such is the light of *emes*. Just a little bit of light can illuminate much darkness.

The time period of the *nes Chanukah* was a time when the very future of Torah was threatened by a way of life so alluring and attractive that it represented the thickest darkness conceivable; one camouflaged in an illusion of light. The intellectuals of the world were espousing the most obscure falsehoods disguised as the truth. It was as much a war of words as it was on the battlefield.

It was a time when the *tehorim*, the *tzaddikim*, and the *oskei Sorasecha* were clearly outnumbered, a time when the speakers of truth were in the minority. However, Hashem was so impressed by those loyalists who stood up courageously for the sake of Hashem and His Torah — by those who were unwilling to be fooled by the attractiveness, the *noy* (a perverse reversal of the word Yavan, *osiyos noy*), who would not allow truth to be twisted and authenticity to be spun — and wrought a miracle on their behalf. In the end, the mighty fell to the weak, the many to the few, the impure to the pure, the wicked to the righteous, and the wanton to the diligent students of His Torah.

We hope and we pray that Hashem will send the *siyata d'Shmaya* so that truth will triumph and *kiddush shem Shamayim* prevail, that the murderers of the innocent will cease to exist and the perpetrators of slander and falseness come to an abrupt halt, that all the darkness will dissipate and the minority of yesteryear become the majority of a new world enlightened by seekers of the absolute truth, and that from that small remnant of pure oil there shines forth a brilliant light that will illuminate the world as Mashiach leads the way to the epic time of acknowledgment and proclamation that *Hashem Elokenu*, Hashem our G-d (a truth recognized by *ehrliche Yidden* throughout the ages) will become *Hashem echad*, the recognized one G-d of the entire united world.

CHAPTER 12

THE RELIGION OF SPORTS

STATISTICS FOR ETERNITY

A husband and wife had been shopping at a large mall most of the day when the wife realized that she'd completely lost track of her husband. After searching all over, she finally called his cell and said, "I've looked everywhere. Where are you?"

He replied, "Honey, remember that jewelry store where you saw the matching diamond pendants and became all emotional about them but I couldn't afford 'em then, so I swore I'd get them for you someday?"

The wife, feeling admiration for her thoughtful husband and happy inside, said, "I do remember that, dear."

"Well, I'm in the sports bar right across from that shop."

THE popularity of sports throughout the world is widespread and has made its mark among our people as well. The evolving of the Super Bowl into a *gantza yom tov* replete with parties and celebrations before and after, with a special menu graciously provided by the local take-out (don't you worry — kosher is readily available!) underscores the significance of this championship game in the eyes of the American sports fan. On the radio, seasoned analysts discuss the particulars of the game that was, or will be, with great fanfare. Every detail is analyzed and taken apart. Should they have replaced the pitcher, pinch hit the batter, allowed so-and-so to play in spite of his injury, or "is this one on steroids?" are just a few of the many topics. A whole *shakla v'tarya* evolves as callers call in with their well-thought-out positions. In many a stadium today kosher food is available, and one can even join up with a regular *minyan* for *Minchah*.

We can thank the Yevanim for this influence as well. Not only were they the forerunners of the universities (with all due respect to the many positive contributions of the *chochmas umos ha'olam*) and all of the decadence that evolved in its wake, but they were strong proponents of athletics and the worship of the body. The Greeks took games of all kind very seriously but especially those that involved physical agility and athletic competition. They believed that their gods particularly loved to see strong, fit, and graceful human bodies. To get on the good side of the gods, one needed to exercise, to eat right, and to oil his skin to create a beautiful physique that the gods would love. Because of the Greek tendency to turn everything into an *agon*, competition, there were invariably numerous athletic rivalries in Greece. The most famous of these is the Olympic Games that the world follows so passionately today. (How ironic that the name for the Israeli national basketball team is Maccabi, the very name of the Chashmona'im who stood up to fight the influences of the Yevanim, an acronym for *Mi chamochah b'elim, Hashem*.)

As one who grew up as an avid sports fan and participant in many a basketball, baseball, and football game, I would like to make a disclaimer. I do understand the importance of exercise and the positive outlet that playing ball can be for a child or young adult. I readily admit that there could be many worse extra-curricular activities in the world that are replete with decadence and promiscuity.

However, I draw a line of distinction between playing sports and sports fans who follow its every detail, engrossed in it day and night. I make the following observations from an idealistic point of view of what Hashem would prefer from us and what we should therefore strive for.

In a nutshell, Hashem wants us to grow up and face life for what it really is. He wants us to put aside the playfulness of our youth and channel it to Torah. "*Lulei Sorasecha sha'ashuai* — Were it not for Your Torah, which is my plaything and delight,"[90] Dovid HaMelech extols. He wants us to recognize the truth of *Olam Hazeh* and *Olam Haba*. He wants us to accept the yoke of Torah and mitzvos as the foundation of our existence in both of these worlds.

In order to so, we must establish priorities. Ideally, those priorities dictate the use of the mind to focus on *yedias haTorah* (and all of its glorious details), rather than the knowledge of every nuance of the statistics of one's favorite sport. Those priorities champion talking in learning rather than the nightly sports wrap-up. They demand that *gedolei Yisrael* become our heroes, and not, *l'havdil*, famous athletes.

I am reminded of a story about the Super Bowl:

> *Bernie was shocked to see an empty seat in the row ahead of him at the Super Bowl. Feeling somewhat bold, he asked the woman seated next to the empty seat, "Excuse me, but whose seat is that?"*
>
> *"Oh! That's my husband's seat," the woman replied.*
>
> *"Well, where is he?" Bernie inquired, perhaps overstepping his bounds. "He'll miss the kickoff!"*
>
> *The lady answered, "Oh, he passed away!"*
>
> *"I'm terribly sorry," Bernie lamented, silently scolding himself for allowing his curiosity to get the better of him and acting so nosy. But never one to control his mouth, he persisted. "Excuse me for asking one more question. Didn't any of your relatives want the seat?"*
>
> *"Oh, no!" the lady answered. "They all insisted on going to the funeral!"*

---

90 *Tehillim* 119:92.

Misplaced priorities, you might say, at its worst. Yet, at times we are not far behind in our distorted hierarchy of priorities and preferences. Growing up in America, we continue in the ways of the ancient Greeks and develop many loves and interests, all of which quickly become part of our very being. Parting from them or even relegating them to a lower position on the chart becomes quite difficult, if not impossible. It is inconceivable to establish a true measure of one's priorities when everything is important. This is amplified by the fact that we live in an environment in which people are accustomed to getting everything and wanting it all. Invariably, this leads to a situation where the truly crucial areas of life are unfairly shared with the less significant ones.

The Chiddushei Harim said it best. The Gemara in *Sanhedrin*, in the course of discussing the issue of *yehareg v'al ya'avor* — when one must relinquish his very life rather than transgress a prohibition, cites the *pasuk* of "*v'ahavta es Hashem Elokecha b'chol levavecha uv'chol nafshecha uv'chol meodecha* — You should love Hashem your G-d with all of your heart, with all of your soul, and with all of your resources."[91] The Gemara proceeds to *darshen*, infer: "*b'chol nafshecha* — with all of your soul, *afilu notel es nafshecha* — even if that love of Hashem, at times, demands that one relinquish his soul."[92] This *drashah* serves as the source for one's obligation to surrender his life rather than serve idolatry (the antithesis of love of Hashem).

The Chiddushei Harim suggests homiletically that perhaps a similar *drashah* could be made regarding the accompanying words: "*b'chol levavecha*, with all of your heart, *afilu notel es levavecha*, love Hashem with all of your heart, even if it means one must give up his heart (and all its many loves)" for the sake of *ahavas Hashem*.

Yes, indeed! One must even give up the Super Bowl for the sake of a higher priority, such as his afternoon *seder*. He may have to give up Dunkin' Donuts for the sake of maintaining his parents' *minhag* of observing *chalav Yisrael*. He will have to put to pasture his previously

91 *Devarim* 6:5.

92 *Sanhedrin* 74a.

cherished choice of entertainment and relaxation because it doesn't meet with proper Torah standards.

Whereas the previous generation, much to our sadness, was subjected to *nisyonos* in the realm of "*b'chol nafshecha*," challenges of actual *mesiras nefesh* where many courageously gave up their lives *al kiddush Hashem*, the essential *nisayon* of our generation might very well be of the "*b'chol levavecha*" variety. In our generation, the primary challenge facing us is that of giving up our hearts and relinquishing our grasp on the numerous playthings of our American youth in order to prioritize our lives, once and for all, in a focused and orderly fashion. When we do this, we will have finally defeated the Yevanim that are *nikbetzu alai*, gathered around me, and continue to surround me, to this very day.

Chapter 13

Subtleties and Half-Truths

Enemies in the West, North, South, and East

Finally, home early from work one evening, a well-respected local surgeon was relaxing on his sofa watching the evening news when the phone rang. The doctor answered it and heard a colleague on the other end. "We need a fourth for our poker game tonight," said the friend.

"Very well. I'll be right over," whispered the doctor.

As he was putting on his coat, his wife asked, "Do you have to go? Is it serious?"

"Oh yes, quite serious," said the doctor gravely. "In fact, three doctors are there already!"

THE most dangerous lie is one that has the appearance of truth. It is easily repeated and is manipulative as it displaces trust with cunning. Similarly, the most dangerous enemy is one who appears to be your friend. "Beware of *reshus*, government (be circumspect of your reliance upon them)," the Mishnah in *Avos* declares.[93] They could appear as your friends when they need you and sell you down the river when they don't. Yet, we tend to become very comfortable as we snuggle up to the nations of the world and try to curry their favor.

> *The story is told of the knight who was reporting on the war effort to the king. "Your Majesty, we have vanquished your adversaries in the south; we have removed the menace from the east; we have annihilated the opposition in the north; and we have absolutely demolished your enemies in the west."*
>
> *"Enemies in the west?" asked the king. "I don't have any enemies in the west!"*
>
> *"Well," replied the knight, "now you do!"*

We are forever grateful for the freedom we enjoy in the West that allows us to observe our religious practices without concern of persecution. America and other democratic nations have been good to us in granting and protecting our religious freedom. To be sure, though, we would be naive to think that we are free of enemies. Anti-Semitism is on the rise in the West. ISIS has shown its ugly head internationally, and in a growing number of democracies throughout the world, Jews can no longer safely walk the streets wearing a *yarmulka* on their head.

Having said that, our greatest enemy in the West, however, is the very freedom that we enjoy. It is this freedom that has contributed to a spiritual holocaust of catastrophic proportions. With all due respect to the awe-inspiring Teshuvah Movement, assimilation continues to spiral out of control. Whereas in the past Jews were scorned in certain typical gentile settings, today, in the spirit of "tolerance" and "political correctness," they are enthusiastically welcomed and unfortunately fall prey to integration.

---

93 *Avos* 2:3.

Prophetically, Yaakov Avinu warns us to beware of Esav when he acts like our "brother," as indicated in his prayer: "Save me from the hands of my brother, from the hands of Esav."[94] What appears to be a redundancy (after all, we know Yaakov's only brother is Esav) serves as a forewarning that when Esav acts like our brother and invites us into his life, he is even a more grievous foe than when he acts like the wicked Esav.

Today, we are bombarded with shells of visual ammunition that pull us into a world where the *yetzer hara* has free reign. And even when that attack is not fully invasive in the physical realm, nonetheless our minds and our hearts are overwhelmingly exposed, at the very least, to a vicarious secular existence powered by a formidable foe.

The more embracing their invitation is, the more loving, the more comfortable, the more precarious the threat. And the more similar their lifestyle is to ours, the more we are fooled into thinking that we share the same value system and behaviors. The more we are deceived to imagine that we can live in their world and survive.

This form of genocide began with the Yevanim. "*Ufortzu chomos migdalai* — And they breached the walls of my towers." They broke down the barriers and said,

> *Come join us. Absorb our culture. You are welcome to experience real living. We also value truth.*[95] *We also have thinkers, philosophers, sophistication, and erudition. We are descendants of Yefes, an expression of yofi, beauty. We are the "beautiful people." Why don't you throw away your archaic practices and get with it? You'll like it so much better. We don't want to kill you, as others did. After all, we are brothers. Let's travel together.*

This notion, rejected by Yaakov Avinu, became an overwhelming challenge for his children in the time of the Chashmona'im and remains as a thorn in the side of authentic Jews until this very day.

---

94 *Bereishis* 32:12.

95 The Rambam writes that Aristotle came close to it.

Let us hope that we will have the strength of the Chashmona'im of yesteryear to stand up against adversity, to see through the subtleties, and understand that Klal Yisrael is not only destined to be an *am levadad yishkon*, a nation that must live alone, but that it cannot survive any other way.

CHAPTER 14

SHOCK TREATMENT

A PARADIGM SHIFT TOWARD MASHIACH-CONSCIOUSNESS

An elderly woman went to the doctor, a new partner to her medical group in town. After about four minutes in his office, she bursts out of the examination room, arms flailing and yelling. Spotting her regular doctor, she explains her bizarre behavior and tells him what happened. The doctor angrily marches down the hallway toward his younger colleague. "What in the world is the matter with you?" he asks. "That woman is almost eighty years old. Why would you tell her she's expecting a child?"

"Does she still have the hiccups?" asks the young doctor.

THE emphasis on the idea that we live in the epoch of Mashiach is no longer solely the discourse of Chabad *chassidim* or religious settlers in the West Bank. It is the talk in every *beis medrash*. With so many signs that point to *chevlei Mashiach*, the pangs of the time of Mashiach, with so much travesty in Klal Yisrael, with so many *nisim v'niflaos* seen before our very eyes (from the Six Day War in 1967, where the Egyptian air force was destroyed without ever getting off the ground, to the 3,500-plus missiles shot at cities all across Eretz Yisrael at innocent civilians that either missed their mark or were intercepted by the Iron Dome in July 2014), there is much reason to anticipate his imminent arrival.

In some Jews, this Messiah-consciousness has brought about a paradigm shift in their religious allegiance. The raised consciousness that the end is near should have a positive effect on all Jews. Unfortunately, too many are like the character in the well-known story of Barry, a secular Jew, who was running late for his job interview in Manhattan. Nervously, he circled the streets looking for parking, berating himself for not leaving home earlier. He couldn't afford to lose this opportunity. As the 9:00 a.m. interview approached, in desperation, with only a few minutes to spare, he offered a prayer to Heaven: "G-d, if you help me find a parking place, I promise I'll go to synagogue every Saturday!" Suddenly, a car pulled out of its spot right in front of the office building he needed to enter. Barry swiftly pulled in and said, "Forget about it, G-d! I found a spot myself!"

The Yom Tov of Chanukah has a special connection to the days of Mashiach. As the last of the Yamim Tovim (in addition to the *Shalosh Regalim* and Purim), Chanukah closes the era of Yamim Tovim until *l'asid lavo* when the third Beis HaMikdash will descend from *Shamayim*. *Az egmor* — then I will complete the *Chanukas Hamizbe'ach* begun on Chanukah. The very letters of the *dreidel* — *gimmel*, *nun*, *shin*, and *hei* — equal the *gematria* of Mashiach: 358. Somehow the *nes* of Chanukah is the bridge to fill the gap until Mashiach's arrival.

Indeed, the Chanukah menorah remains as a *hemshech*, a protraction of the lighting of the menorah in the Beis HaMikdash.[96] There is a *segulah*, auspiciousness, in those *licht* that helps to inspire and confirm within us our belief in Mashiach's arrival. This is hinted to in the *berachah* to Yehudah that describes the arrival of Mashiach and the assemblage that will greet him as *ad ki yavo Shiloh v'lo yikhas amim* — until the arrival of the *Mashiach* when nations of the world will gather to pay homage to him.[97] *Yavo Shiloh* has a *gematria* of 358 (like the word *mashiach*), and in

96 Ramban to the beginning of *Parshas Beha'aloscha*.

97 *Bereishis* 49:10.

the continuation of the *pasuk*, *lo*, to him, has a *gematria* of thirty-six, a *remez* to the thirty-six candles of Chanukah.

What exactly is it about Chanukah *licht* that helps to bridge the gap between the last of the Yamim Tovim until the great celebration of the ultimate redemption in the days of Mashiach? Those lights represent the light of the Torah in the face of darkness. They symbolize the only tool that has allowed, and will continue to allow, the crossing of that bridge to that glorious day as Klal Yisrael traverses the dangerous paths of *galus*. There is much light to look forward to at the end of the tunnel, but Torah is the light in the tunnel itself. Its symbol may be conspicuously missing from many a Holocaust Museum, but we know the truth of our survival and we dare not forget it.

In a *shailah* posed in Rabbi Yitzchak Zilberstein's *Veha'arev Na*, the quandary is cited about a man who was doing *hagba'ah*, the lifting of the *sefer Torah* during a *Shacharis minyan* in the town of Netivot when the sirens went off. What would be the proper *kavod* for the *sefer Torah* in such a scenario: to leave it on the *shulchan* and run to the shelter, or to take it with him, even though that would mean removing it from the *beis hakeneses*? Rabbi Zilberstein opines the latter (unless carrying the *sefer Torah* would place its carrier in greater danger) as the prohibition of removing a *sefer Torah* from the *shul* is not applicable when the purpose is to protect the *sefer* itself. In this case, should the missile hit the shul and cause a fire, *chas v'shalom*, the *sefer Torah* might be destroyed.[98]

If I may take poetic license and disregard for a moment the *psak halachah* in the unfortunate circumstance of the scenario of this *shailah*, I would venture to say: There can be no question about whether to take the *sefer Torah* into the shelter or not, for the *sefer Torah* is the very shelter we seek, and the medium with which to access the salvation of Hashem.

The *pasuk* that ends the *haftarah* on *Parshas Chazon* says it all: "*Tziyon b'mishpat tipadeh v'shavehah b'tzedakah* — Zion will be redeemed with judgment and its captives returned with righteousness." *Tzion b'mishpat*

98 Rabbi Yitzchak Zilberstein, *Veha'arev Na*, vol. 2, *Parshas Va'eschanan*.

tipadeh has a *gematria* of 1,076, which is the exact *gematria* of *Talmud Yerushalmi*; *v'shavehah b'tzedakah* has a *gematria* of 524, which is the exact *gematria* of *Talmud Bavli*.

In other words, the redemption will come through the study of *Torah Sheba'al Peh*. *Baruch Hashem*, we have seen in our time a proliferation of the learning of both *Shas Bavli* and *Yerushalmi*. This too is a sign that we are close to the *geulah sheleimah*. Torah has been that beacon of light in the face of darkness that shines forth from those thirty-six beautiful *licht* and will continue to light up the path *ad ki yavo Shiloh*, *b'vias go'el tzedek bimheirah b'yameinu*.

CHAPTER 15

WHAT'S IN A NAME?

TOV SHEM MI-SHEMEN TOV.

The charming and dashing presidential candidate confidently entered the nursing home with his entourage and approached an elderly lady in a wheelchair. "Good morning, ma'am! How are you today?"

The old lady didn't give him the time of day. "Ma'am, do you know who I am? Do you know my name?"

Again, the old lady all but ignored him.

Speaking a little louder this time, he said, "Ma'am, are you sure you don't recognize me? Do you know my name?"

"No, I don't know your name," she replied, "but if you go to the front desk, I'm sure they can help you find it!"

THE Gemara tells us regarding Rabbi Meir: *dayak b'shmah*, he exhibited caution with respect to a person's name and thereby avoided lodging in a certain inn whose proprietor's name connoted dishonesty.[99] In fact, the holy books tell us that parents, when naming a child, are inspired with a spirit of *ruach haKodesh* of sorts and that the chosen

99 *Yoma* 83b.

name reflects the essence of that child and his potential. At the *bris*, all proclaim: "Just as he entered the *bris*, so should he enter to Torah, *chupah*, and good deeds." The very name one is given at his *bris* will directly reflect upon his ultimate accomplishments in life's most crucial areas of Torah, marriage and family, and good deeds.

The *mishnah* discusses whether it is proper to administer two punishments (monetary payment and thirty-nine lashes) for one violation. In contrast to the opinion of the *rabbanan* that the *pasuk* dictates that one does not receive two punishments (*kol hameshalem eino lokeh*, all who pay do not receive lashes), Rabbi Meir insists that when the source of each punishment is a separate *pasuk*, both penalties are to be administered. He states: "*Shelo hashem* — For the Scriptural verse that is the source (the name) for the punishment of lashes is not the same (name) as the one that is the source for monetary payment."[100]

It is interesting to note the use of the word *shem*, name, to mean "source or origin." One's name and the reputation that he builds during the course of his lifetime are inseparably linked to his origin, to the root of his *neshamah*, to his uniqueness and individual portion in Torah as one of the 600,000 *neshamos* of Klal Yisrael. His name is a hint to his purpose in life, as he strives to equate his earthly performance with its parallel heavenly expectation. Indeed, the numerical value of the word *shem* is 340, the same as the numerical value of the word *mekor*, source (spelled without the *vav*).

How unfortunate it is that so many, merely for the sake of blending in with their Western culture environs, have abandoned their Hebrew names in favor of these names' English counterparts. The *Yiddishe numen*, Jewish name, is reserved for and often only invoked at special occasions like the *bris*, bar mitzvah, and eulogy. The Jordans and the Scotts, the Jessicas and the Jackies abound all around us. Even more unfortunate is the loss of perspective of one's purpose in life and personal mandate from Hashem. There is a source to his existence, the calling of his *neshamah* to be revealed, and his real name is a Heavenly

---

100 *Makkos* 4a.

ordained hint to that mandate, if not a constant reminder that there is a task to be done and that only he can do it.

The *Ne'os Hadesheh* writes that the reason one cannot fulfill the mitzvah of counting the *Omer* simply by listening to his friend count for him (through the concept of *shome'ah k'oneh* — one who listens is considered as if he said it) is because the counting of the *Omer* is a prelude to *kabbalas haTorah*, which must be unique and exclusive for each and every Jew.[101] Every Jew has his own individual portion in Torah, and his *kabbalas haTorah* must reflect his acceptance to fulfill his personal requisite. It has been said that there are 600,000 *Yidden*, 600,000 letters in the Torah, and 600,000 interpretations for every verse in the Torah. The very name Yisrael is an acronym for *yesh shishim ribo osios l'Torah* — there are 600,000 letters in the Torah, a composite of 600,000 unique portions, each individually designed.

The Greeks made every attempt to sever the personal relationship that each Jew has with Hashem and the Torah by issuing a decree: to write on the horn of the ox, *she'en lachem chelek* — that you don't have a portion with the G-d of Israel. They decreed that we proclaim on the very instrument we employ to awaken our special inner link and bond to Hashem — i.e., the horn of the ox, the shofar that we blow on Rosh Hashanah — that we have no special portion in Hashem and His Torah. And although we defeated the Greeks, the victory was not complete; their influence continues to haunt us to this very day.

Consider the following:

- *Koheles* tells us: "*Tov shem mishemen tov* — A good name is better than good oil."[102]
- Torah and mitzvos are compared to a candle and a light, respectively, as it says: "For a mitzvah is a candle, and the Torah is light."[103]

---

101 *Ne'os Hadesheh*, 1:197.

102 *Koheles* 7:1.

103 *Mishlei* 6:23.

- A person's soul is likened to a candle as well, as it says: "Man's soul is Hashem's candle."[104]
- The Torah itself is called *tov*, good, as it says: "For I gave you a good teaching; do not forsake My Torah."[105]

With all this, perhaps another explanation can be suggested for the *pasuk* in *Koheles*. The phrase *mishemen tov* can be understood not as "better than good oil," but rather as "from good oil." This means to say that a good name comes from good oil, and good oil is one that burns well and produces light, namely, the fuel and fire of Torah and mitzvos, represented well in the Chanukah menorah (the twenty-fifth word in the Torah is *or*, a *remez* to the twenty-fifth of Kislev). A good name — that is, using one's name to actualize his potential and uncover his purpose in life and personal portion in Hashem's Torah — comes from *shemen tov* — the brilliant oil and light of the only *tov* that exists, i.e., the Torah.

A Jew must peer deeply into the Torah to identify himself and then his name will become renowned in both this world and the next, as he will have uncovered his unique *shoresh haneshamah*, root of his soul, while striving to equate his earthly image with its spiritual projection above.

---

104 Ibid. 20:27.
105 Ibid. 4:2.

Chapter 16

Sing and Thank Hashem for Everything

Baruch Hashem yom yom.

After saving up for many years, a rabbi decided the time had come to purchase a new automobile. He entered the local new car dealer's shop and was quickly spotted by the salesman.

"Have I got a car for you!" the salesman exclaimed, unable to conceal his delight at finding an obviously religious Jew at his dealership.

"What do you mean?" the rabbi asked in apprehension.

"Let me show you the latest designed computerized digital commands," the salesman replied. "You will not believe your eyes! You see, this car has no pedals to accelerate and brake!"

"But how do you stop and start?" the rabbi asked, somewhat baffled.

"Here, get in and I'll show you. Ah! That's the beauty of this baby. With this new Israeli computerized technology, all you

have to do is speak and the digital processor will instruct the motor what to do," the salesman explained. "Now this particular car was designed for the religious consumer," he continued. "Just watch this. To start moving, I simply say, 'Baruch Hashem.'" With those words, the engine began to hum and they were on their way.

Amazed at what he had just witnessed, the rabbi asked, "How do you stop it?"

"That's no problem!" answered the salesman. "All you have to do is say, 'Shema Yisrael,' and the car will stop immediately." And sure enough, the car rolled to an abrupt halt.

The rabbi, decidedly impressed, bought the car. Entering his new prize, he said the magic words, Baruch Hashem, and the new engine hummed as he headed out to the local highway. Soon, the rabbi had left the city behind, and was cruising along the winding country roads, enjoying the beautiful scenery along the way. Caught up in the enjoyment of his new toy, he veered off the main road at a fork, failing to notice a sign warning that the road was closed. Before he knew it, he had ascended a half-completed bridge. He recognized that he was in grave danger and close to falling off the unfinished open end of the bridge into the water below, and he instinctively reached for the brake pedal, but there was none to be found.

Then he remembered that this car was different, but in his state of panic, he could not remember the right words. What do I say? What do I say? His mind was a blank as the car bore down on the end of the unfinished bridge and an inevitable plunge to a traumatic and watery demise. Preparing for his last moment on this earth, the rabbi declared, "Shema Yisrael!" as he had never said it before. With those words, the car screeched to a complete stop, the back end resting on a tilt, the nose leaning precariously over the side of the bridge.

The rabbi, soaked in perspiration, removed his trembling hand from his forehead. Aware of the amazing miracle that had just occurred, he exclaimed with deep feeling, "Baruch Hashem!"

CHAZAL entreat us to say *Baruch Hashem* in all situations. Even at the most difficult junctures in life, we are instructed to bless Hashem with the same enthusiasm as we would bless Him at times of joy and prosperity.[106] This philosophy of life is built upon a strong belief that all that HaKadosh Baruch Hu does is ultimately for our good as "He bestows His goodness on good and bad people."[107] The question is therefore not, "Why do bad things happen to good people," but rather, "Why do good things happen to all people?"

The answer, of course, is because the *Ribono Shel Olam* is completely good, and whether we understand the reason for an event or not, it is nonetheless always for our good.

Hillel the Elder epitomized this belief. Whereas Shammai the Elder would always put aside the finer animal he might find during the week for Shabbos, Hillel trusted that when *erev Shabbos* would come, Hashem would provide for him. As the Gemara says: "But Hillel the Elder applied a different standard, for all his actions were done for the sake of Heaven, as it says: 'Blessed be my G-d day by day.'"[108] Although Shammai's approach — preparing for the Shabbos from the first day of the week — is preferable for most people, Hillel had an extraordinary amount of faith and did not want to infringe in the slightest way on this crucial foundation of life of blessing Hashem each and every day according to the events of that day. To have food set aside for Shabbos would have implied a lack of *emunah*, faith in G-d, to provide his daily sustenance. Perhaps more importantly, it might have weakened Hillel's resolve to always be cognizant of Hashem as the ultimate Provider each and every day.

Divine Providence is not haphazard or inconsequential. It is not occasional or at one's whim. It is ongoing and is with meticulous calculation;

106 *Berachos* 54a.

107 Rosh Hashanah liturgy.

108 *Betzah* 16a; see Rashi.

it is built on a modality so sagacious that it eludes the comprehension of our limited faculties:

- It could be something as simple as the time I rolled down the window of my rented car in the Katamon neighborhood of Yerushalayim, totally lost, and the first person I encountered just happened to be a young married woman whose family had spent summers with us in our bungalow colony. Not expecting to meet anyone I knew in that neighborhood, or even recognizing her, I was shocked when she responded to my quest for directions with, “Rabbi Kurland, is that you?”
- Or it could be something as consoling as that terrible day when we finally brought my critically ill mother, *a”h*, to the oncologist, who confirmed the dreadful suspicion. The doctor felt that my mother should go to the hospital immediately. It was his last appointment of the day and he asked if he could hitch a ride with us there as he needed to make his rounds. In the car we began to schmooze, and my mother, even in her weakened state, participated in the conversation as well. We soon discovered that this doctor had once lived in Harlem, where my *zeide* had been a rabbi. It turned out that the doctor had grown up in my *zeide*’s shul and remembered him well. My mother never stopped talking about the *chizuk* that she felt from the *hashgachah pratis*, Divine providence, that this doctor whom we had chosen actually knew her father and was now to hopefully become the messenger to help bring about her recovery. (She did, in fact, recover, and lived two more years.) It gave her strength to know that the *Ribono Shel Olam* was watching over her. Indeed, she never stopped saying *Baruch Hashem*.

Chanukah is a Yom Tov that was established to remind us that this is what we Jews do, *l’hodos u’l’hallel*, to give thanks and to praise. This is our response to all questions and all situations. We are ever so thankful to Hashem who created us and the world around us *yesh me'ayin*, matter from nothing, watches over our every move, and grants us the gift of life in this world and the next. And for this we are eternally grateful and proclaim with sublime joy, *Baruch Hashem yom yom* — Blessed is Hashem every day."[109]

V'kavu shemonas yemei Chanukah eilu l'hodos u'l'hallel l'Shimcha ha-gadol!

109 *Tehillim* 68:20.

About the Author

RABBI Yehoshua Kurland has warmed the hearts and souls of hundreds of students throughout his forty years as a Rebbe and *maggid shiur* at Sh'or Yoshuv Institute of Jewish Studies in Far Rockaway, New York. As a long-time student of its founder, Rabbi Shlomo Freifeld, of blessed memory, Rabbi Kurland has absorbed into his bloodstream much of his famed Rebbe's teachings and shares them — with a touch of humor! — in his popular lectures and books. His last book, *A Time to Dance* (Mosaica Press, 2016) inspires all of us to better relationships and was an instant bestseller.

Born and raised in Baltimore, Maryland, Rabbi Kurland lives with his wife, Leah, and family in Far Rockaway, New York.